MW01040343

DEREK'S GIFT

A portion of royalties and publisher proceeds
will go to the Derek Sheckman Foundation
and toward battling cancer.

To watch Derek's video visit:
www.DereksGift.com

Derek's Gift

Gift

A True Story of Love, Courage and Lessons Learned

Michael J. Tougias
and Buck Harris

FEATURING
Derek Sheckman's Journal

NORTIA
PRESS

Orange County, California

NORTIA PRESS

www.NortiaPress.com
2321 E. 4th St., C-219
Santa Ana, CA 92705

Cover design by Roslyn Crowell.

ISBN: 978-1-940503-08-0
LCCN: 2014936215

For author speaking engagements please contact the author at:
michaeltougias@yahoo.com

For all other information please contact the publisher at:
contact@nortiapress.com

Printed by Worzalla in Stevens Point, Wisconsin, USA

Contents

Introduction

VALERIE AND DEREK WERE FRIENDS FIRST. GOING BACK TO 7TH GRADE, their paths naturally crossed as all the town's elementary schools came together for the first time. "I remember the first few weeks of gym class in middle school," recalls Valerie, "and the instructor had the girls and the boys line up according to height. I was next to Derek." As they counted-off to decide teams, they were picked to play the same position but on opposite teams.

Derek later said that was the day he fell in love. Valerie said she remembers feeling flattered. She knew he liked her. She thought he was cute (in that middle school kind of way) but hadn't felt more than that. What she didn't know was that this 7th grade courtship would blossom first into a beautiful, strong friendship and then later into a deep-rooted, powerful connection that would change her life.

When they entered high school their last names placed them in the same home room and next to each other in some of the same classes. Consequently, they saw each other every weekday. Both played fall sports and would see each other on the playing fields after school; soccer for Derek and field hockey for Valerie. During Junior year they sat next to each other in Spanish class and this is where Valerie remembers things changed for them. Although both were very driven students in the honors program, they looked forward to their time here. Valerie recalls her seat was in front of Derek's and that anytime the teacher turned away he would do something to make her laugh. Valerie no longer thought Derek was just another guy in her class but instead looked forward to seeing him. She loved how his eyes lit up when he smiled. He had also grown much taller since 7th grade, and now was a lanky 5'10", playing both varsity soccer and basketball.

There was a growing connection between the two and a natural ease, but they were not yet boyfriend and girlfriend. The catalyst for that transition was a birthday phone call from Derek during the summer before their senior year. It wasn't just any phone call—Derek had to do a little planning and make a real effort. He was touring Israel that summer, and when he took the time to call Valerie from halfway around the world, she was overwhelmed that despite all the new things he was doing and seeing on his trip, he thought of her. And she missed him. It made her think that Derek would be more than just a friend. And when he returned from Israel, the two became a couple, and their relationship was one that started like any high school romance.

But that was to quickly change. Derek was diagnosed with cancer five months later. Their typical high school relationship was no longer simple. It would be much more. It was extraordinary, but I'll let Derek tell that story in his own words.

Chapter 1

Derek's Journal

This journal is for all the people who know me and everyone that does not. It is for the members of my family, both immediate and distant. It is for all of my friends, old and young alike. It is for my teachers, mentors, and coaches. For my fellow teammates, Israel trip members and board members. It is for fellow classmates, club members, and class officers. It is for my doctors, surgeons, technicians, specialists, and nurses. It is for those who have been or who are cancer patients, it is for the young child or elderly person who was just diagnosed with a serious illness. It is for those who have or will experience surgery, from a simple tonsillectomy to heart bypass. For those who have experienced the death of a loved one. It is for everyone and anyone. The intention is to inform and educate. It is to dispel any secrets, rumors, or misunderstandings. Ignorance is not bliss, rather knowledge is power. It is one chapter in a long and wonderful score. Here is my story.

Derek's Gift

January 22

So much has happened in the past few weeks. I don't know where to begin. It was the very first of the month when I began to have pain. It started as what seemed a mere toothache—right lower tooth, I made a trip to the dentist and there he told me that I may have TMJ caused by grinding of my teeth at night, so he gave me a plastic mouthpiece and I wore it for a few nights. I felt confused, as I had never had this type of problem before. As the days passed, the pain slowly began to intensify. It was this weird feeling in my right jaw—an aching feeling and it was getting worse. I saw an ear, nose and throat specialist because I had also felt a sore throat earlier in the month. This did not go away either. My father, the doctor, became alarmed and decided to set up an MRI yesterday for me to rule out anything serious. It was the first time I have ever been in that machine—the MRI. It was kind of scary—They put me in this small tunnel, where I could not move. And there were these loud banging noises. While I did not become claustrophobic, the whole thing just creeped me out. When it was over I was relieved—I thought I would never have to do that again.

I was in school today, calculus class to be exact, when the phone call came. I knew it was for me —I just knew it. I was told to go to the office where I found out I would need to go back to the MRI and have some follow up tests. Something was wrong. I could feel it in my bones and I could feel it in my jaw. So I went and had another MRI and they put contrast in my veins to help enhance the images. I was uncomfortable once again but this time I was much more anxious, knowing that something was up. My father took me aside. I sat down in what seemed a rock hard chair. He told me today that there is a mass that has grown in the massater space near my right jaw, causing the pain I have been

4

experiencing. He said it could be benign or malignant, and would have to be removed by surgery. When I heard this, a million things raced through my head. Tears of fear engulfed my being and a dark malaise grew over my soul. The news hit me like a ton of bricks. Feelings of anger, rage, sadness, and fear overtook my very existence. I was scared out of my mind: scared of death, scared of what was to come, scared of the unknown.

January 23

I had several tests done today. We went to the Union Hospital in Lynn. I had a CAT scan of the head, neck, and chest. They made me drink this white chalky stuff—it tasted awful. It was another type of contrast. With all the advancements in medicine today, you would think they would think of a way to administer me contrast without having to drink awful white chalky liquid.

Today all of my questions started to surface as I bombarded my dad with inquiries about this mass in my head. However, he could not provide much relief, as much of what was happening was just as new to him as it was to me. I missed school today. I haven't told anyone about what was happening. First because I was in no state to discuss it and second, there were still so many unanswered questions. The mass, or tumor as it is called, may be benign or malignant. Could it be? No it couldn't be... cancer... could it? I also missed basketball practice—the coach is going to kill me. Somehow I have a feeling I'm not going to be playing for a while though. I thought a lot about Val lately. We have been fighting as of late and our relationship is about to end. All of a sudden, everything we have been fighting about is unimportant. I really love her and I need to tell someone about what is happening. The results of the tests today were encouraging. No sign of any other abnormalities or masses in my body.

I went back to school today. My close friends asked me where I've been and I just shrugged them off. I started taking painkillers to take the edge off, I couldn't drive to school. I'm hiding all of this from everyone—I don't know quite how to handle all of this. I can't go to basketball practice today.

Nothing new to report today. The last few days have been very nerve-wracking. I have never felt so confused or scared in my life: The worst part is that I myself don't know what's going on. It is a time of total and complete chaos. Also, I can't tell anyone because... well because I don't want to tell anyone.

Can't write anything too substantial today—it feels like someone is constantly hammering against my head. I can't even get up and walk around now. School is long gone—haven't been there in what seems like ages. Can barely sleep and eating is near impossible. Can't write anymore. Gotta lie down and rest. I can't believe this is happening.

Went to see an otolaryngologist (ear, nose and throat) doctor at Mass General Hospital. He gave a quick examination and looked at my recent MRIs. When he returned he began to discuss my options. He said that I could let it grow until it eventually killed me or I could have it removed. I worried about this day ever since I found out what was in my body. He explained the removal procedure—a mandibular jaw split. An incision would be made from the lower lip down to the neck and then the jaw would be pulled away exposing the tumor, which would then be removed and my jaw shut back together. When he told me this, my stomach turned and I felt sick to my stomach. I glanced at my parents and began to cry—crying was not something that I did often. The only thing I could think of was that incision he described and the way it would make me look. I could not get it out of my mind. I felt like I was in some kind of movie and the "bad" music was playing—only it was real and incredibly scary. I thought to myself, it's not worth cutting up my face, and then I rationalized it and realized this was my life we were talking about. The doctor explained that before any of this was done, they would need to biopsy the tumor, to be sure that it was benign as they suspected it would be. They would do a needle biopsy, going through my mouth and taking a piece of the tumor to analyze. If the tumor is benign, they would go ahead with the surgery to remove the mass at the same time. If the tumor is malignant, they could not remove it because attempting to take it out might cause more problems than I started with. If they pulled out a cancerous tumor, there is a large chance that the action alone would cause it to spread. I was told that the chances are that this mass would be benign, be removed and that would be the end of it. I hope to God that is all it is. I can't stop thinking about Valerie—I need to tell her how much I love her. I need to tell everyone what's going on. I can't hide this anymore.

February 23

I can't believe what I'm about to say, I have cancer. I have recently learned that the mass that is growing is a rhabdomyosarcoma, a rare form of cancerous tumor. Rhabdomyosarcoma is a soft tissue tumor that arises from muscle cells. It can arise anywhere in the body, but is most common in the head and neck area. Rhabdomyosarcoma is extremely rare, as "there are fewer than five new cases for every one million children in the United States each year" (National Cancer Institute). The placement of my particular tumor is also extremely rare, located in the masseter space behind the right jaw muscle, making me "one in a million." I think it will take some time to let the idea sink in. You see, when I first woke up from the anesthesia of the biopsy, I was not aware of what was going on. All I remember is asking my dad, "Did they get it out?" and he said they had not. I remember feeling relieved that there would be no scar when I woke up. It was not until I was awake that I was told I had cancer. In a way I was relieved. There were no scars and I finally knew what was causing my pain. I wanted to know right away how I would be treated, for how long, and what were my chances to live. My mind raced with so many emotions they could not be counted. I couldn't believe this was happening. The first thing I thought of was me having no hair. I know, it is superficial, but I could not shake the image from my head. I was going to be one of those people, the kind of people you always saw and looked the other way. You felt bad for them but were somehow scared of them also. That them is now *me*, the they are now *I*. I think of my childhood friend in elementary school who had cancer. He was out of school for so long and missed so much. He lost his friends and everything else, I remember not thinking too much of it at the time. I felt bad for him but was never that close to him, I was also very scared of the whole thing. Now I know that was because I was scared of what was foreign to me. I remember how sick he looked with no hair and cringed at the thought of looking like that.

I stayed in the hospital for quite sometime. I got my own private room. About two or three days after the biopsy, the phone calls and the cards and the flowers and the gift baskets started arriving. That meant that people were finding out that I was sick and that I have cancer. It helps to write it down—I know it's real if I do. I never had to tell anyone that I was sick. Everyone already knew. It's amazing how quickly people find something out and it spreads even quicker. I thought of Valerie and all my other friends and how they would react. I thought of how I would react if this happened to them. I hope that my friends will stay my friends. I'm worried about being and feeling alone. I don't want to be one of "those people"—but I am. I soon met my new oncologist. He introduced himself. He seems very kind and gentle. I like him. He spent a long time with us (us being me and my parents) discussing the treatment plan. When he was telling us all that was about to happen to me, I went into a kind of dream state. I blocked out all that was around me, including the doctor's explanation. I just kept thinking, "Is this really happening to me?" I was later explained the treatment for this type of cancer involved intensive radiation and chemotherapy. Surgery (removal of the tumor) had been ruled out because of the difficulty of the location of the tumor. The chemotherapy would include three separate drugs: cytoxan, actinomycin, and vincristine and would be administered over a 40 week time period. Every three weeks for a year, I will go into the hospital to have these highly powered and toxic drugs whose sole purpose was to kill all remaining cancer cells. However, the drugs will kill all cells, both cancerous and normal. I will therefore have many side effects.

February 24

Because I am going to have so much chemotherapy, they decided to put a catheter to administer all the drugs and take blood biweekly. A catheter is a soft, flexible, hollow tube that acts as a more permanent IV. There are definite advantages to having the catheter: with the amount of times that I will receive drugs and have blood taken, I would have to be stuck with a needle thousands of times.

February 26

There is absolutely no question in my mind whether I am going to survive. I am assuming that I will get my treatment, and then I will be free of this disease. Death is not an option. I never want to know what the risks of the treatment are. I do not want to hear the negatives, just the positive. While this is a good outlook, some may say that I am being ignorant, that I am not paying attention to what is physically happening. I just want to be well again. I must keep a very positive feeling through this or I know I will never survive.

February 27

I can't imagine what all this is doing to my parents. Their little baby is sick and they can't stop it. I know they feel powerless and frustrated. They have been there for me every step of the way. Never leaving me alone when I needed someone and ready to be out of the way when I am with my friends and feeling better. Sometimes I think my age is the worst age for something like this to happen to someone. Kids who are younger do not fully grasp what is going on. But someone my age—it is very difficult. Because

I am 18, I am part of the decision making process. I decide what treatment I will receive and what I will do with my life. I would like to be in charge of my health, but in a way I like being a kid. I don't have to explain stuff to everyone—my parents can do that for me. I like having my parents there next to my hospital bed to be there if I get real sick. There is something very comfortable and soothing about my parents. The thing is this: if this disease that has stricken me is in fact a genetic problem, my parents have to feel somewhat responsible. I am not saying that I am blaming them or even that I think that is the case: I can't help thinking that, though, they are responsible. The thing is, I love my mom and dad with all my heart. I am so lucky to have two loving parents who have helped me through by far the hardest days of my life.

March 2

I went back to school today for the first time in almost a month. I know that everyone at school knows what has happened to me. It is a small town and a small school and things get around quickly. I am beginning to look different. I shaved my head real close so that when my hair starts to fall out, it won't be traumatic to watch it. I know that most people know that I'm sick, but don't know the whole story. Many people tried their best to treat me normally, while others tended to shy away from me. I think those who said nothing to me were scared not of me, but more of the disease. I understood this feeling and did not blame anyone for feeling the way they did. I think most people did not know how to act around me. Most of the kids my age were not afraid really of the disease—they knew that it was not contagious. However, I think it is part of the human psyche to be afraid in that way. English class was the hardest for me. It is a class where we sit in a circle for discussion. You can see everyone and more importantly everyone can see you. It was impossible for me to concentrate on the task at hand. All I could think about was what has happened to me over the last month and how people are going to react to me in the months to come.

By far the worst part of chemotherapy was the sickness I felt after each treatment. I was nauseous beyond belief, feeling lethargic and just dead. After a week's time I would usually start to rebound and feel much more normal. It was tough knowing in advance that every three weeks I would feel so awful, I would have to plan my schedule around how I was going to feel. The concept that these drugs were doing good, not evil was extremely hard to grasp.

The people at the hospital were so helpful, considerate, and understanding. The nurses were all very helpful, especially my primary nurses who were always checking on my progress. But the hospital had an air about it that didn't sit right with me. I don't know if it was the disinfectant smell, the endless white hall ways, or the feeling of being around really sick people, it became harder and harder to go there every three weeks!

But I did it, and I did not complain. I have to give myself credit where credit is due. Throughout this whole ordeal, I was very compliant. I was a very good patient, I did not want to cause a lot of trouble. I wanted to do what was necessary and then leave. I don't think everyone could have handled it quite as well. This is probably due to my relaxed temperament and laid back personality. I am not bragging by any means, but I think I handled myself well. Part of the reason I was so compliant was that I did not have much of a choice: I had to go through the radiation, the chemotherapy, and later the surgery. The alternative was death and to me, that was no alternative. This was something that I thought about a lot. Everything I did, I did because I had to. There was no thought of any other action, except to get better.

March 8

It is so good to be home from that hospital. I spent so much time there. I am hoping that I will not have to spend so much time there in the future although I have a bad feeling about that. I mean, what is going on inside my body is anything but normal. They keep telling me how rare my disease is. I am scared but I know there is a light at the end of this tunnel.

March 10

It is amazing how many people have been affected by this. I have received cards and gifts from so many people. It is like that six degrees of separation thing. I affect a bunch of people and each one of those people affect another bunch of people. It's weird how it works that way.

March 11

I have received so many cards from so many people. I got flowers, stuffed animals, candy, cookies, food, prepared meals, gift baskets, balloons, and an infinite amount of cards. There are people who have sent me things whom I don't even know. Each day I become more aware of how many people's lives I have touched. What is most amazing is that I haven't received one duplicate card in the million.

March 16

I was thinking today about how many people have been involved in taking care of me. Just in that one hospital stay, there were hundreds of doctors, nurses, technicians, surgeons, and doctor's whose titles I did not know or understand. They were all there to take care of me and to help me. That was very comforting though.

March 18

Being a teenager, I am very self-conscious of the way I look—every teenager is. Losing all my hair, and I mean all my hair, all over my body, makes me look and feel different. It is like a brand stuck on me that says "he's sick, so stay away from him." What makes me look most different is the loss of my eyebrows and eyelashes. It makes me realize that there are many things in life that you do not appreciate until they are gone. It feels as though everyone is staring at me, not knowing how to act or speak to me.

March 20

It's weird how something becomes more apparent once they are right in your face. Before I got sick, I did not notice how much there was out there. I watch TV and all I see and hear about is cancer and more about cancer. I don't think that there is now more out there, I'm just much more aware of it now. I wish I weren't though. Why did this happen to me and why now?

March 30

Something happened last night that was truly amazing. I am at a loss for words. I love Val more than anyone else the world.

14

April 3

Today I learned the details of the next step—radiation therapy. Through the use of two different radiation beams, the tumor will be in a sense burned away. The first radiation beam is used at the Mass General Hospital. The second beam will be administered in Cambridge at a special lab on the Harvard campus. The MGH beam will take about 10 minutes every day for a couple of weeks. That means we have to drive into Boston every day to get this very short radiation treatment. That's really gonna mess up my schedule. I won't be able to get anything done. And my mom will have to miss a lot of work. I hope she doesn't lose her job. I have a long road ahead of me.

April 5

Went out last night with my friends to watch the fireworks. I was feeling well, almost normal. We hung out at Alicia's house until the fireworks. Then we walked the entirety of Puritan Road, which for me would have been a trek, but I was fine. The fireworks were beautiful. I held Val in my arms as we watched, thinking how lucky I am to have her. What a girl!

April 20

I have had a couple days of this radiation already and to tell you the truth it is really not that bad at all. It does not take too long and I'm out of there. I am feeling a little better now too. You see, they stopped one of the chemo drugs during the radiation. Apparently that particular chemo drug does not react well with radiation. As a result, I am not feeling so shitty all the time. This is the first time in a long time that I have felt ok—just ok.

April 30

Radiation is still going on as planned. I know I said things were easy here and that it was not a big deal—but things seem to be getting harder—or I'm just getting frustrated with it. Every day my mother and I have to park at MGH and walk in the building and then wait and wait and wait and sometimes wait some more. Then they call me to be treated and it takes ten minutes and we are on the way home. But it just takes away a large chunk of the day. I go after school and when I get home it is later in the evening. I'm getting sick of commuting to Boston each day. I don't know how people do it. I would go crazy.

May 4

I have finished with one part of the radiation—the beam at Mass General Hospital. I feel a sense of accomplishment. However, I have such a long road ahead. I am not looking forward to this next part. It is called the Harvard Cyclotron. It is a special radiation beam using photons instead of the more conventional proton beam.

May 10

I have been thinking a lot about my brother lately. He is important to me. For the past few years he has been sick as well. He has become a different person. However, I continue to look up to and admire him. Sometimes I feel that I am being selfish with my sickness. I feel like I want to do something to make my brother better—but there's nothing I can do. I look forward to a day when we are both sitting talking about our different experiences and remembering them as bad memories—that's it—just bad memories. He is one of my driving forces for getting better. He needs me just as much as I need him.

May 14

I am at the age when the kid is supposed to prepare to leave the nest, become independent, meet new people and do new things. I will not be able to do any of that. I have officially decided to take a year off and postpone my enrollment at Tufts University. It's funny. The day I received the letter that I had been accepted early decision was the day I had that first MRI. This is the best move for me right now. I will still be going through treatments and I will not be looking my best in that first fall semester. So I will take the year off. I will plan on first of all getting better and back into shape. I will also probably work or try to get an internship. I am looking forward to this year off from school. I do need a break. And the possibilities for what I can do are limitless. I will have a little time to myself also, which I need desperately. I need time to work things out—think about stuff—get my head together. And when I go to Tufts I will be a new, healthy person ready to take on the world.

May 18

God is a hard subject to talk about because I have been questioning his existence my entire life. How can I believe in a God when all of this shit has happened to me over the past few months. If this was meant to happen, then why the f____ did it happen to me? I have been wrestling with this thought ever since I was told this news. When I was little, I used to believe in God for very different reasons. As I grew older, it became impossible for me to believe.

I am a very practical person and a very scientific person. Only black and white makes sense to me not the gray in the middle. I remember going to Temple when I was young and wondering why I was there. What was the purpose? I began to get older and being Jewish became more of a family tradition and not a religion. It was a way for my family to connect throughout their many generations. When I went to Israel, I was confused even more about my religion. However, since all of this has happened, I just find it incredibly hard to believe. It's extremely hard to believe. It's f___ing unbelievable to believe.

May 20

I love being by myself. I love having no one to talk to. No one to entertain. No one to amuse. Just me, myself, and I. I love being left to me and my thoughts. I'm not really a loner, but I like a lot of quiet time. Maybe that's why I don't like hanging out in a big group. Maybe that's why I enjoy the company of a couple of people—the small crowd.

May 24

I am done with radiation and I have this huge sense of accomplishment. For six weeks I have consistently been through hell and I came out ok, l am so glad that I'm done. No more schlepping into Boston every single day. I am finished and damn proud of myself. No more radiation and I'm more than halfway done with chemotherapy. I am beating this thing and I am getting it done. I am the man. I can't believe how relieved I am right now. No more feeling uncomfortable and no more sitting still for hours at a time. They gave me a certificate to congratulate my finishing and it was the most rewarding piece of paper I have ever received. Things are good. I am feeling better than I have in a long time. I am fighting this son of a bitch and I am going to win. The next week should be so much fun. Senior week which includes the prom, banquet, parties, and graduation is next week. I will be feeling well because chemo was almost a month ago and radiation is done. I'm excited for next week. Things are good.

May 29

Last night's prom was unbelievable. We had such a good time. My tux was looking good, my date was beautiful, and the night was spectacular. Everything went according to plan except a small screw up with the disc jockey. Someone forgot to confirm him. Besides that everything went great. The whole night was perfect. I was feeling really well and everyone was treating me normally and I danced the whole night. Valerie looked so gorgeous, like an angel. We had such a good time together. We went out after the prom and had a great time too. We stayed up all night and hung out with who we wanted to hang out with. The best part was that I felt so normal. I don't think I thought about being sick once the whole night.

June 9

There is something about graduation that was so incredibly gratifying. It's not just the end of a high school career but a sign that I can accomplish anything if I put my mind to it. I can even graduate, be a speaker, pass my AP exams, be VP of the National Honor Society, while being sick with a life-threatening disease. I so enjoyed leading the way as the four officers marched their way to the stage. I felt somehow important and sad that it was ending all at the same time. Somehow this graduation meant so much more to me than I ever would have thought before I became sick. It meant that despite my being sick, I was able to get through what I needed to accomplish—a great feat. I was able to give the concluding speech and lead my fellow classmates in the ceremonial throwing of the caps. Getting my diploma was just indescribably awesome. And seeing my closest friends receive theirs was even better. And when it was all over, I was so very saddened. It was like everything was coming to an end. All my friends would soon be leaving for school and I would still be here. I felt alone and confused. I went back to the field where the graduation took place because, believe it or not, I had forgotten my diploma, and I looked out at all the empty seats and bleachers, and really felt like a huge part of my life was over. But I put on my face and went to all the parties I could before I became tired. The whole last week has been such a joyous time with the prom, cookout, banquet and at graduation. I am feeling better than I have in a very long time. My hair has even started to grow back. I stayed out late after the prom and did all the normal things that teenagers should do. Sometimes I would forget that I was even sick at all. But I am worrying about what is going to happen next.

June 10

My family and friends have been so amazing. I am so lucky to have their constant support. They are calling. They are writing. They are cooking. They are doing anything and everything to help me. I appreciate it more than they know. I love them for it. That is the truth. After last week during graduation it became even more evident how many people are out there cheering me on.

Graduation was a great day and I have been thinking about that lately. I have been thinking about this for quite some time. I love each and every person who has been there for me.

My family has done everything in their power to help me. They really have done everything and for that I am grateful. I also need time to myself. It is part of my personality. I need to be alone especially when I am not feeling well. I don't like for people to see me when I'm sick. I'm not much fun to be around and I don't need the extra anxiety and pressure. It is the way I want to handle this and I think, no, I know people understand. It is the way I have wanted it and the way I will continue to want it. I understand, though, that it is not fair to keep people away. I will do my best to remember that as long as they do the same. I am just so impressed by everyone.

June 27

There is a fine line that my parents have had to live on. That is, they must give enough space so as not to smother me, but not leave me alone—especially while in the hospital. They are learning but never seem to get it right. It is not their fault, though, because I am unsure of that fine line just as much as they are. What I would really like is to be totally independent. I am 18 years old for God's sake. I need my freedom!

July 10

I dread that overnight in the hospital when they pump me full of drugs and I know when I leave the hospital, it will be a long while until I feel well again. That is another strange thing about this. When one gets sick they do not know its coming, so they do not have to anticipate feeling shitty. I have to get ready every three weeks to feel sick. This means that I have to schedule everything I do by this three week schedule. When someone asks me to do something, I must think to myself, will I being feeling well or puking my guts out that day. I hate that. And my schedule affects my parents schedule and everyone else's schedule.

August 24

Alex left for school today and I somehow feel empty. I am going to miss him so much—he has no idea, I know that he will keep in touch regularly, but it won't be the same. We hung out last night and when we dropped him off, I said goodbye. I broke down crying. He has been such a large part of my life for so long, and now he is gone. Most of my friends have already left or are leaving soon. Val goes to school soon too and even though she will be close by she will not be three minutes away anymore and I won't see her every day. Alex and I were together every day and now we will see each other every couple of months. It's gonna be hard to make that adjustment. It will be especially hard for me because I will be home not doing anything. At least he will be at school meeting people, going to classes and having fun. It's really hard to watch all my friends go away while I am left behind. I don't know what I'm going to do with myself. I think I will enjoy some time to myself though too. It will give me time to think and to get my ideas together for next year. I'm really going to miss everyone, though.

September 1

Val left for school today. I'm hoping that she gets there ok and that her roommates aren't obnoxious slobs. I really want her to be happy there. I think she will be but I'm worried. I feel responsible for her going there and I should feel responsible. She was going to go to Syracuse until she decided this summer that she wanted to stay by me. In a way it was good, because it made her realize that she should do what she wants to do, not what anybody else wants her to. She is an amazing artist. The sculpture she made for my birthday is absolutely incredible—it is truly amazing. I'm gonna miss seeing her every day though. I love her a lot. She's one of those special girls that you have to hold on to.

September 15

People don't appreciate the simple things in life. This comes from the movie *Awakenings* with Robert De Niro. A great theme throughout this movie is this concept. People really don't appreciate the simple things in life: friendship, feeling well every day when you wake up, eating your favorite food, taking a walk on the beach. The list goes on and on. The point is that there are so many who don't take advantage of the things they have in life. I didn't realize this until these things were taken away or made harder for me. My advice is take advantage of the simple things. Appreciate what you have and understand how easily these things can be taken away. I am jealous of all my friends who have it easy or so it seems to me. I am so envious of them. I have to believe there is a reason for all of this though. There has to be.

September 17

I have recently started to feel some slight pain in my jaw. The pain is reminiscent of before I was diagnosed with cancer. Day by day, it seems to be getting worse and worse—just like it did in the beginning. For the first time, I am really scared about what is going to happen. Something is wrong—I can feel it all through my body.

September 22

Today I went to the hospital to have an MRI. When the results came back to the doctor, he informed me that the tumor had started to grow again. The chemotherapy and radiation had not done its job and the cancer was getting worse. I then learned that I would have to have surgery. I knew at that moment that my life was about to change dramatically. I was pissed off because they had originally told me that the tumor was inoperable. Now they were saying that it is able to be removed. My first thought was excitement that finally this thing that has been causing me so much pain and suffering was being taken out. Get the little f___er out. It was not until our appointment with the head and neck surgeon that I realized the magnitude of what is going to happen to me. The surgeon told me to remove the tumor, they would need to cut into my face, pull the skin back, take the tumor out, and then put the skin back. The thought of the whole thing made me sick. I am so worried about this surgery. I do not want to have scars all over my face. I will look ugly and disgusting— but it will save my life. Why am I forced to make decisions like this? Why can't I be like everyone else and worry about normal teenager problems.

September 23

My parents and I decided to get a second opinion on the surgery.

We went to see Dr. Ivo Janecka—a specialist in skull base surgery! His explanation was much like the first doctor's. He seemed to know what he was talking about, though. It was then that I knew that this would be no simple procedure. Two doctors agreed on the same type of surgery and there was nothing easy about any of it.

October 2

I'm going in tomorrow to have surgery and I am scared out of my mind. I am scared of how I will look, how I will feel, and how I am going to handle this whole thing. It's like this is my last night of normalcy. I feel as though I need to go out and do something outrageous before my life changes. My life will never be the same after this. Please let me get through this.

October 14

I have just spent 10 days in the hospital post surgery. I came home today and it was so good to be home. Home really is where the heart is. These past ten days have been the darkest days of my life. The surgery took 15 hours. They performed a facial translocation in which a team of several surgeons cut into my face—on the nose to below the eye to my right temple, down near my ear and across my neck. They pulled the skin back, removed the bone that goes from the temple to the lower jaw, and removed the tumor. Then a separate team reconstructed my face. They took a flap of muscle from my stomach and put it in the open space that my tumor once occupied. I spent many days in the Intensive Care Unit. It was the most awful experience of my life. Val came to visit every day even though she had a ton of work to do, she made it over every single day. This was one of the many ways that I knew she really loved me. I did not want her to see me the way I was in the hospital. I was just ugly. Big scars all over my face—my eye sewn shut, a big piece of plastic hanging out of my nose, skinny as a rail. But she kept coming back to the hospital until I let her see me. And that first time I saw her there was this amazing sense of relief that the worst part was over. I saw her smiling face, gave her a hug, and smelled her amazing smell—the one that was so familiar to me.

October 15

I quote Tom Petty: "You don't know how it feels to be me.".No one in the whole world can understand what I am going through. They can try to help me and comfort me, but they just don't know how it feels. I wish I could find someone—just one person—who has experienced what I have experienced, but there is no such person. My case is so unique and I feel alone. This realization has just come to me. Before when I was going through chemotherapy and radiation, there were others experiencing the same thing. But now, it is totally different.

October 16

I have been at home now for a couple of days and the reality of what has just happened to me is starting to settle in. I can't believe what I have just been through. I am clear now on the fact that I have a lot of recovering to do—probably the biggest recovery in the history of all recoveries. I keep looking in the mirror to see what I look like and I am still surprised. I am telling myself that it will look and feel better, it will just take time. Time heals all wounds. I am not so worried about what it looks like, rather how it feels. The whole right side of my face is numb. It's that feeling you get after you have Novocain at the dentist—only I have that feeling on the whole right side of my face. I must show everyone including myself that I can do this—but why does it have to be so hard?

October 18

I believe what doesn't kill you makes you stronger. If that's true, I am really, really, strong.

I found out today that my dad's significant other has moved out of their house for good. I know they had been on the outs for quite some time but I never questioned it. I was too busy thinking about other things. Our relationship was never that great, but I always liked her for this important reason—she kept my father happy for a long time and for that I thank her. I somehow feel responsible though and therefore have mixed feelings. Yes, she and I were not the best of friends but, she made dad happy. Now my dad is lonely and must go through my recovery by himself. I am hoping that he finds someone soon.

October 19

I am very worried about this numbness I'm experiencing. It's amazing how you don't realize how important something is until it is gone. Things would be so much easier if I could feel my face. There's also this sense that I am not in control of my body because I can't feel part of it.

October 21

If I had just one wish it would be to have feeling in my face again. I try to talk to people but they can't understand me—it is the most frustrating thing in the world. You want to communicate something and you can't. I feel so limited in what I can do. Eating is hard too. I have to keep wiping my mouth to make sure nothing is there. I can only chew on my left side so I have to take smaller bites and that means I eat really slow. I am also not very hungry. I think my stomach has shrunk or something. I eat to please my mom and not because I am hungry. I force food down to try to gain weight. I am very skinny—probably the lightest I've ever been. I want to gain weight but I can't force food down.

October 22

My face will permanently feel uncomfortable and will permanently look different. There is something about permanence that is so scary. Permanent means that it will never change and will be there forever. This is the reason more people don't get tattoos. They know the tattoo will always be there—even when they are old and wrinkly, and they will regret having it done. It is the same feeling here. If I had to go through this for a certain amount of time and then it was over, it would be a different story. When I had chemo and I lost my hair—yes it was traumatizing—but I knew my hair would eventually come back and I would feel the same again. Now, post surgery, what has happened to me is permanent and I can never change what has already been done.

October 26

People don't realize how lucky they are to be healthy. I watch TV and see all these perfect faces and I want so desperately to be like them. I've never wanted to be someone else until this surgery. My self-esteem is gone. I used to have this normal cockiness about myself. I thought I was invincible. I thought I could have any girl if I tried hard enough. No that's not true. But I felt good about myself. Now all I can think about are these stupid scars and how ugly I look. Sometimes I feel like that. But a lot of the time I am very optimistic. I keep telling myself that I am going to keep looking better. One day these scars will be so faded people won't even notice them after a while. Someday my life will get back to the way it once was. Life will never ever be the same.

October 28

If this damn tumor were anywhere else in my body, I would not have to go through all of this. Why couldn't I have had it in my leg or my arm or my chest? Why did it have to be inside my head? A person's face is so important. It's what the world sees. Everything else can be covered up somehow, but not the face. A person's face represents everything about them. You see a picture of someone, you look at their face. You talk to someone, you look at their face. You do anything and you look at their face. Well, my face is deformed forever. It will always look different.

November 23

I have just spent two and a half weeks in the hospital and I am pissed. It was the most frustrating experience of my life. You see, on Halloween night I fainted on the way to the bathroom. It was a great night before that, though. Val was home from school and we got to be together, which I love. The next day l was checked into the hospital to be monitored. They brought me to the intensive care unit and I stayed there for several nights. I began to have dizzy spells, which I guess I had been having before but didn't really realize it. It was determined that something was wrong with my heart. No one knew what and why this was happening to me.

After days and days of being very uncomfortable, they finally figured out that I was having ventricular tachycardia—an electrical disturbance in the heart causing me to have several extra heartbeats. I know now that when I fainted I had a long run of these extra beats at once and that caused my heart to race and me to faint. So I was back in the hospital, AGAIN. I was there from something that seemed to have nothing to do with the cancer. Another unrelated health problem that would keep me down. I was so angry I wanted to punch something—but I didn't have the energy.

I know that I will never really be well again. Too much has happened to me. The thing about the heart problem is that it's just another thing that's keeping me from being well. It will keep me down. I will have to take heart medication probably for the rest of my life. I will not be able to really exercise or do anything athletic again. It used to be such an important part of my life and now it's gone. It's hard for me to accept that. Not just because of the heart but because of the extensive surgery I've had. I can't play soccer or basketball with any kind of the same fire I used to. That part of my life is over. But I loved that part. It was part of me.

Of course Val was at the hospital visiting me every day. Even though she had more work than she knew how to handle, she jumped on the T and took a long ride to the hospital just to see me. I knew that it was a large pain in the ass to come see me, but she did it anyway. And when she was there I was happy. She made me smile. I knew that she loved me because of the things she did for me and I will forever be grateful for that and I will forever love her. My parents continued to stay with me in the hospital. I felt bad about them missing work and being there doing nothing. But I know they love me so much, they have also shown that as well. Not that there was any doubt before. And I love them too.

November 25

I thought about many things being in the hospital for over two weeks. One thing that I haven't addressed lately, is the whole God issue. After the surgery, I was more confused than ever about this alleged great being. Maybe God made me sick, or something else made me sick and somehow God made me better. But it's really not God. It is a bunch of surgeons with scalpels. I just want to know why. Why me?

November 27

I was informed while in the hospital that Brian Desroches' dad died of cancer recently. He had been battling the disease for quite some time now. I am so sorry for their family. He will no longer be in pain, though. Their family has been through so much. People like us do not deserve this kind of pain in their lives. It scares me to death. I could be him someday and my family would have to deal with that. And what about Val? I just won't think about that. I gotta be positive. Positive thinking has gotten me through so far.

November 28

Thanksgiving dinner has come and gone again. It was so very good to see the whole family. There was something familiar and comforting about being around the ones you love and the ones who love you. Dinner was excellent, just how I like it, all my favorite foods. It was one of the first times I had been out since surgery. I tried to get dressed up and look my best but it was hard. I had the new tinted glasses on and the cover up makeup to try to hide the scars.

The family has been so supportive-through all of this. I have so appreciated everything they have done. I know that I have pushed them away and they have been very understanding. It's not that I don't or didn't want them there, but I often did not feel well enough to deal with a lot of people. They should know how much I love them. I don't know what I would do without their support I love them so much. I really want to name them each individually and that's exactly what I intend to do. In no particular order: Mom, Dad, Brother Bryan, Papa, Nana, Grandma, Grandpa, Uncle Richard, Alice, Aunt Marilyn, Uncle Herb, Uncle Ed, Aunt Dorothy Lazurus, Aunt Muriel, Cousins Greg, Jennifer and Steve, Meadow Rose, newborn Gabriel, Brother/Best Friend Alex, and Fiancée Valerie. These are the members of my immediate family and I felt the need to mention them. I love you all so very very much.

December 1

Even though I had such a long and grueling stay in the hospital these past few weeks, there is also something comforting about being in a hospital. In a hospital, you know that everything will be ok. It's like a safety blanket. If something goes wrong they can fix it or make it better. If I have pain, they can take it away. I quote Morgan Freeman in *The Shawshank Redemption*. Talking about prison, he said, "There's something about these walls. First you hate em'. Then you grow used to em'. Then you learn to depend on them." It is the same feeling for me with the hospital. I am an institutionalized person. I feel safe there and I don't know whether I can make it on the outside or not.

I just watched the show *Party of Five*. Charlie, the oldest sibling, has learned that he has cancer. It is too familiar. In this episode he started his radiation therapy. They showed the machine and it was again all too familiar! It brought back a lot of bad memories. I keep thinking if only my cancer and my treatment were that easy. The six weeks of radiation were by far the easiest six weeks since I was diagnosed. They're making a huge deal out of this and compared to me, he has it so easy. I guess everything is relative, though. One's relative happiness can only be compared to what one has experienced before. The cold has given me a nasty ear infection in my other, healthy ear. I can't hear a damn thing now. I used to get ear infections as a little kid all the time. Maybe that's the cause of the cancer, the ear infections. . . or the medicine I took for the ear infections. What am I talking about! Well it could be, it could be anything I did.

December 12

I do not know what the future holds for me. It's amazing how what has happened to me in the last year has changed my whole thought process. College used to be so important to me. The idea of college was important to me. So many things were different I was doing everything that I was expected to be doing and everything that everyone else in a rich upper middle-class town was doing. I still think it's important to be educated. It is probably the most important thing in the world, except for love. Advancing and learning is the whole basis of society. But that does not mean I have to go to Tufts and be the normal all American white boy. I am in no way, shape, or form. . . normal. I feel in so many ways that I am too old for college life. I'm not saying at all that I am a genius and do not need to be educated. But after what I have been through, there is no way that kids at school would understand, and I don't expect them to. I can't go on now and pretend this has not happened. At least before surgery, I would have been able to put this behind me. Now I am scarred for life, both mentally and physically. My whole life is just so different I am truly and utterly confused, I need more time to think.

December 14

Today I went to Val's mother's art opening at her gallery. It was really good to get out and I enjoyed it. Val's mother is extremely talented and I can see where Val gets her artistic qualities. Leslie's artwork to me is just amazing. It's something I respect her for and am impressed by. It is so nice to have a passion and to be good at it too. Val's whole family has been just incredible throughout this whole thing. They are the reason that she is able to deal with all that has happened. The whole family, they have really taken me in and treated me well. I love Valerie and they know that. I know that they know that I did not mean for this to happen. I did not want to put Val through all this heartache and pain. I just love her and I will always love her. I will always love Leslie, Ken, Nikki, and Mike for everything they have done. Just wanted to say thanks.

December 15

It is Monday and a new week is here. Alex is coming home soon as well as everyone else. I am worried about seeing people but more about people seeing me. The left side and the right side of my face look like they belong to two different people. Sometimes I wish the surgery hadn't been done at all. At least then I wouldn't feel so uncomfortable and look so different. But then I realize that I would have died without this surgery. I had no choice. It's too bad that I had to make this decision so early in my life. It's not fair. It's just not fair.

December 16

Val and I went out for dinner last night and talked a lot about what has been going on. I told her that I know that I am not going to live a long life. If I live to my thirties I will be surprised. It is a feeling that I have. I do not have cancer anymore, but I am still very sick. I have heart problems; I have potential infections brewing in my face and head. I have a weakened immune system from chemotherapy. I have a very good chance of getting cancer again. And I will not fight it again. I do not have the strength.

December 17

I have no energy and I can't do anything substantial without having to lie down. I have not been well for so long. I have not felt good for so long. I remember when feeling well was something that I just expected. It is something people take for granted. Being healthy is a gift in my mind. I recently felt bumps on my head and they are getting bigger. I have a bad feeling about all this. I just want to feel well again. That's all I want in the whole wide world.

I know that if the cancer spreads or I get it again later in life that I would never be able to go through the treatment process again. My body couldn't handle it and my psyche couldn't handle it. You see, if the cancer does come back it is something telling me that, for some reason, I was not supposed to live a long life. I still believe that everything happens for a reason. Maybe it's so that my close friends or family can devote their lives to cancer research to find a better way to treat and cure cancer patients. Maybe it's so those close to me learn to grieve and make them stronger people. Maybe it's to tell Lance to stop smoking. Maybe it is so that Val can find happiness somewhere with someone some day. And maybe I'm just really unlucky and this whole thing f____ing sucks.

December 20

I am dying. The cancer has spread and I am going to die. Yesterday after a long day seeing various doctors I was informed that the cancer has spread to my chest and kidney. It may also have recurred in my jaw and may be many other places including my eye, face, and head. The doctor informed me that the cancer had spread and that my chances for living were very very slim. I was told that every case is different, but I did not have much time left. Maybe a few months. Maybe a year. I think I was in complete shock—utter and total shock. My first thought after I heard this news was Val. I thought of how much I love her and care about her. She means everything to me. I had to tell her as soon as I could. She is my best friend in the whole world and me the same for her. I thought of everything we must do together and how much I wanted to marry her. Although I won't ask her to marry me. It would not be fair to her. In a way the news was also relieving. I am so uncomfortable all the time. I feel sick almost constantly. I do not want to feel this way anymore. I want to be happy and this is not happy. On the way home from the hospital a million things went through my head, I thought about my family and friends. I am so worried what this is going to do to people. I feel like I'm abandoning people and there's nothing I can do about it. My brother is already severely depressed. What will this do to him? And my parents, who have been there for me since the day I was born. I don't want them to be all alone in this world and be sad and depressed for the rest of their lives. But most I'm worried about Val. She has been my everything for so long and I love her so much. I wish she did not have to go through all this pain. She deserves to be happy. She is the most special, amazing, intelligent, beautiful, awesome, caring, sensitive and every other adjective person in the world. I feel sorry that I have put her through this pain. I never meant to hurt her. I love her so much. I love her so much. You know, this wouldn't be so hard if there weren't people left behind who love me. While I am sad for myself and just keep wondering why this happened to me, I am in tears for all those around me that must pick up their lives and move on after I am gone. I never thought I would have to write this kind of stuff down. It's like it's not real, like it's some kind of movie. I only have a certain amount of time left and that is it. I also feel like I must now do everything I wanted to do in my lifetime in this short time I have left. But I know that this is impossible: first because one needs a lifetime to do everything in a lifetime, and second because I do not feel well and I will continue to not feel well. I have to say I knew something was wrong long before the news came to me. I even wrote it in my journal. My body did not feel right and I have been feeling sick. The kind of sick that you can't explain. The kind of sick where you just know something is wrong but cannot pinpoint it to one area. I am not scared to die. I am scared to become very sick. I do not want to be in any more pain. I will be truly happy when I am no longer in pain. That's all anyone wants for another when they love each other— for the other person to be happy. In this case the people that love me will be saddened by my death but will know that I am happy. I have to decide now what to do. There are a couple of options that I must think about. First of all, I could have radiation on the tumor growing in my jaw to try to shrink it so it does not cause me unbearable pain later on. There is also an option to try yet another chemotherapy drug. However, I have been informed that taking this drug will not cure the cancer, rather it will prolong my being sick and eventually dying. My first reaction is not to do anything at all. I do not want to suffer for a long time and these treatment options would just keep me alive for a little longer—not even that much longer. I figure I should take the time I have now—feeling semi-ok and do what I need to do instead of spending my last healthy days in the hospital. Basically, I'm going to get really sick and I do not want to stretch that suffering out.

December 21

Alex came over and I told him that the cancer had spread and there was nothing that can be done. Val was there with me as she has been while I explained to Alex that I was going to die. His reaction was to talk his nerves and fears away. He was shocked by this news. His immediate impulse was for the three of us to go do something really special. So upon my dad's permission, the three of used his credit card to stay at the Four Seasons Hotel last night and just have as much fun as we possibly could. We all figured that we need to get a lot of stuff done in a short period of time.

Material things don't make any difference now. Money has no value. We went for drinks (Shirley Temples) at the Ritz Carlton Bar and then swung back to the hotel for dessert by room service. We had such a good time together. That's what was important. It didn't matter where we were, as long as we were together. The three of us talked about a lot of things last night and into the early morning. We talked about who and how we should tell. We talked about our memories together. And we talked about what I want to happen in the future.

The most important thing to me by far is to make sure that all the people I care about are well taken care of when I am gone. Everyone needs to take care of each other because the people that I love are so important to me—I want them to be safe and happy. I asked Alex to promise me that he would take care of my dearest Valerie once I am gone and hope he holds true to that promise forever and ever. I also asked Val to take care of Alex, my parents, and especially my brother later on.

Val and I had a good long cry last night too. We have become so close and the love we have for each other is indescribable. I don't want to leave her. I know everything about her and she knows everything and then some about me. She's my girl and I'm her boy. She's my honey and I'm her baby. She's my hottie and I'm her shmoopies. She's my cute little package and I'm her love. It's just not fair. It's not fair. I would do anything to be with her forever, I know in my heart that she will go on to live an amazing life. Because I will forever be a part of her, I will get to do all the things I wanted, by way of her. I just don't want her to go through all this, I feel like spending this time with her now is just pushing her deeper into loving me and making it that much harder when I go. But I just can't stay away from her. I love her so much. I love her more than anything in the whole world and I always will.

December 22

I said before that I am not scared to die. That is not true at all. I am scared out of my mind. I don't want to die. I am so scared of becoming sick. I don't know what to expect. I am told that I will be kept comfortable but I am not comfortable now. I don't know the last time I will see those I love and that is a very scary thing. In some ways it's easier to know that you're going to die in advance. I can get everything I need to in order. I will be able to say my goodbyes to everyone.

December 23

Last night was a great night. Alex, Val, and I talked for a long time about what has happened. We discussed many things last night. Alex told me that he is thinking of transferring to Boston University this next semester.

There are many reasons for his decision. U Penn has not had what he wanted for a while now. He feels like the people there are not what he is about. Obviously too, he wants to be near me now in my time of need. He feels that he has missed too much of my life already. If he goes to school here, he will have the support of his closest friends and his family, who will be nearby, after I am gone. BU has everything that he is looking for in terms of academics. He said that with all this happening it puts things into perspective. He should do what he wants to do and not what he is expected to do. Life is too short. He wants to make movies and I think that's awesome. I think it is one example of turning a negative into a positive. It reminds me of what Val has done. She stayed nearby

40

because she wanted to help me through a hard time. But because of that she ended up going to art school and she is doing very well, loving what she is doing. It makes me think that maybe all this does happen for a reason,

I know what Alex has told me is by impulse, like us going to spend a night in a fancy hotel. He is mixing up his devotion to me with what he wants in his life. I think it would be best for him to return to U Penn, where he began a new life. However, even if he decides to stay just this semester and be there for Val, I think that is ok too. They need each other. U Penn will be waiting for him next year.

The two of them are amazing people. They have had such a large effect on my life and me on them. I am the luckiest person alive. Some people never have friends like that in their whole lives. I have touched their lives and I will always be a part of them. It is for that reason that now whatever they do I will be doing it as well. I am a part of them and they are part of me. So all the things I wanted to get done in my life, I will get done—through them. I am hoping so much that they take care of each other. They need each other. For so long I have been their life and that will end soon. I am really worried about them! I don't want to leave them. Why does this have to be so hard? This is a disadvantage of dying slowly. I must watch the people close to me grieve my death when I am still here. I wish I would have just gone quickly and suddenly.

December 25

Val and I have decided to get engaged. We both asked each other at the same time, so it was a mutual decision. We will be engaged but will not marry. We both know in some ways that this might be more hurtful than happy, however we are sure of what we have done. We figure that if we somehow unite as one, that I will be with her all time, symbolically. Plus, I love her more than anything else in the world and have always wanted to marry her. Last night was the first night of Hanukkah and we all lit the candles. We broke out my special menorah that was to be saved until I was married. It was beautiful to light the candles and say the prayers. This might be my last Hanukkah, so it was very special.

December 27

People must realize how lucky they are to be alive and to be healthy—it is a gift. They have forgotten that the simple things are the most important—friendship, love, learning. One must live life to the fullest because you never know when your time might be up. Do the things you want to do and not what others tell you to do. Learn to be your own person and be proud of who you are. This whole experience has opened my mind tremendously. I have learned to be more compassionate and caring. Give time to those less fortunate all throughout the year, both financially and physically. Tell someone in your life that you appreciate them— give them a compliment, it will go a long way. Be open to new ideas (listen to people, really listen), try to look at things from a new perspective. When you find someone you love, hold on to them as long as you can. Be a good person, someone that I would be proud of.

December 28

Music is amazing. I love everything about music. When I am listening to a good song I am taken away into a different world. I feel no pain, just happiness. Some music even makes me dance and for others I cannot hold back humming the words. I used to love to sing and play the guitar. It was another part of my identity that I lost after the surgery. I had trouble speaking (forget singing). A song can make you forget all your worries. Music is just the best thing in the world.

December 31

Today is the last day of a very long year—an extremely long year. The events that have taken place over the last year have dramatically changed my life as well as the many lives around me. Last year at this time, I was a healthy young teenager without a worry in the world. It was the first of January when I first began to feel the slightest bit of pain. Now, a year later, I am preparing to die. I think I have discovered the meaning of life. The reason why we are put here on this earth. That reason is love. I have discovered numerous types of love. There are as many types of love as there are people in this world. I love every person that has touched my life in a slightly different way. I have learned to appreciate people for who they are and I truly love them. But love also hurts. It is love that connects my soul to everyone else's. It is love that will cause sadness and grief. And it is love that will allow me to live on in the hearts of others. I would love to tell each and every person that is close to me that I care about them. However, in trying not to forget anyone, I would like to say this: To all the people who have touched my life and to whom I have touched back—I love you.

January 2

This will probably be the last New Year's that I will experience.

It was the last Hanukkah. It will be the last everything for me because I will probably not live another year. If someone asked me a year ago if I had six months to live, what would I do, I would have had no idea then, and I have even less of an idea now. One of the many things I have learned recently is "carpe diem"—seize the day. One should live in the present, live life to the fullest now. Do not wait to tell someone how you feel abut them. Do not wait for the right moment. Tell people what you want and need to tell them. Seize the day.

January 4

I feel so old, like an old man. I feel old in so many ways. Physically, my body is simply wasting away. I have pain all over: I am constantly taking medication. I walk slowly and I can hear my bones creaking. I need help to do things I once did by myself. More significantly, I feel mentally old. A person's age is not just determined by the amount of years they have been on this earth, but also by the experiences they have gone through. There are ninety year olds who have not experienced half of what l have. It's like I have lived a full life in an eighteen-year span.

January 6

I said before that I love everyone who has touched my life. I feel though that this is not enough. There are so many people out there who have been there for me through everything. People who have unselfishly given themselves to me to help me feel better in my time of need. They have prayed for me. They have cooked for me. They have sent me letters, gifts, baskets, and balloons. They have befriended me. They have put me in as part of their family. They have made an extra effort to make sure I know they are thinking of me. They have given their free time to me. I want you all to know that everything that you have done for me has not gone unnoticed. I really, truly appreciate everything and I love you. I love you. I love you.

January 7

There are lots of things that I want to accomplish in my life. I will not be able to do it all, though. Therefore, I will need those close to me to carry out what I want to do. Not to say everything on my list can be done, but maybe just some of them. Here are some of them: *jump out of an airplane *travel to Israel a third time *be on a game show *ski the hardest trail *travel to everywhere * own a restaurant *own a bed and breakfast *be a gourmet chef *have a large sailboat *be a millionaire *take a trip across the country *gamble in Las Vegas *legally order a drink *see Saturday Night Live in person *have a New York City apartment loft *have fun *play for the Boston Celtics *write a classic novel *help people *design logos *be a caregiver (doctor, social worker) *rent and watch hundreds of movies over a one day period *taste every food in the world once *find an easier way to administer chemotherapy *help cancer patients *get one person to quit smoking *I WANT TO DO EVERYTHING.

January 8

I just want to be left alone. Everything seems to be getting to me. Everyone seems to be annoying me. I'm tired of being sick. I'm sick of being tired. I'm tired of everyone asking how I'm doing. How do you think I'm doing? I'm dying. I don't know what it is that's making me so irritable. I'm sick of everything. I don't want to be left alone but I want to be by myself.

January 12

I love my family and friends and everything that they have done for me. They have sent me constant messages, cards, good thoughts, and everything else. I simply do not want people to see me the way I am. I look very sick. I am deformed. I am constantly not feeling well. I cannot entertain people. I want people to remember me the way I was. That was who I was. I was not always sick with cancer.

January 14

While this journal was originally intended to reflect what has occurred in the last year, the emphasis has changed. There may be therefore some parts that are not as detailed describing the tribulations of my treatment. You see, these things seem so less important to me now. Before I thought that things were going to get better and my story would be an account like many others who have been through what I've been through. I did not want to forget such an enormous part of my life. It is important to document things so that one has a point of reference to refer to. This is why I kept a journal in Israel—to remind myself. I think now I must focus on what my life has meant in the past, what I have done and accomplished. What I plan to do. This past year is one year in the life of many years.

January 16

Time is such a strange thing: the future, the past, and the present.

I have lived almost twenty years. I have been through twenty years of experience, growth, and learning. Yet there is so much I cannot do. I am limited not only by physical incapability now, but also time is running against me.

There are so many things that I want to do and I am hoping that what other people do that know me will carry on my dreams.

January 17

This could be the last entry that I write in this journal. It has been almost a year now since I have started this journal and I am getting worse every day. Every day I am getting worse. I am feeling worse, looking horrible, feeling pain all over my body. Sleeping at night has become near impossible. I have been anxiety-ridden and unsure of what is to come. What the future holds is such a mystery. I feel I should write now while I have the energy and strength. I keep thinking I need to leave something behind. Leave my mark on society—to show that my life has meant something— that it has had some significance. There are the people on which I have and will leave my heart and soul. It's like I need something solid, touchable, tangible for people to see and look at and have a memory in solid form. It's like I have all this money and resources which I should leave behind. I should donate to some organization, some cancer research, leave a building or a laboratory. Help somehow other people or kids that will have to experience what I did to make it easier or somehow more manageable.

I really want to have my life make a difference. I have lived almost two decades and I have done so much. I have experienced so much. Many things that some never do, and never will. But somehow, I feel incomplete. I need to get things in order. I need to go through my past and I must prepare for what is to come.

Make up some kind of will. Make sure the material things are taken care of. I want to go through what I have done in my life and share these things with the people who will live on. I want to tell every single person in my life what they have meant to me. I want to write a separate note or leave a present or tell a secret or story to someone. It is impossible though because there are so many people, so many things to tell, and just so little time. It is for this reason that I must also write down what I want for the future. I have started this but this idea is equally impossible. The possibilities are endless once again.

January 18

I don't want anyone to remember me the way I am now. I don't want to be remembered as the kid who got sick with cancer, went through treatment, lost a battle and eventually died. When people remember me, I want them to think of a healthy young man: strong, athletic, intelligent, friendly, caring, sensitive, loving, honest, handsome, mature, brave, confident, competent, thoughtful, kind, affectionate, musical, and everything else. I am not trying in any way to be conceited or cocky in any way. I WANT TO BE REMEMBERED AS ALL OF THESE THINGS AND NOT THE ONE WHO WAS SICK. THIS IS SO IMPORTANT TO ME. IF WHEN READING THIS JOURNAL, THIS THOUGHT IS THE ONE THAT YOU REMEMBER, THEN I WILL BE SATISFIED.

January 22

It has now been exactly one year since my first entry in this journal, I am getting sicker and my time is short. This is the conclusion of my experience over the past year. I emphasize again

Derek's Gift

that I want to be remembered as a healthy young man and not a man of sickness. It has been one year in the life of me. Two years in the life of a long and meaningful score.

Derek died a few days later on January 28th. He was at home in the arms of his mother, Sandy, when he took his last breath.

Chapter 2

The Next Six Months

VALERIE HAD SPENT THE LAST TWELVE MONTHS BY DEREK'S SIDE, TAKING it one day at a time. Together they tried to support each other through the phases of his illness and decide how to make the best use of their time. All the while she tried to stay as upbeat as possible. Now there was nothing. Emptiness. A black void. She wondered how in the world she would go on. She had no plan, and there were no next steps.

The fact that she knew this day was coming didn't help one bit. Derek was gone. Permanently. She had a mix of dull emotions: relief that Derek was now beyond the reach of pain, and anger that he had left her alone. *How could he leave her?* But mostly what she felt was numbness. The singular purpose in her life had vanished. And purpose, whether dim or strong, propels us forward. Valerie knew that. Even going to Derek's funeral was something to focus on—a purpose, a last goodbye. But now, the morning after the funeral, she wished she could just disappear.

She forced herself to get out of bed and began going through the motions of the day. *First step, make my bed.* Even that felt difficult. Then she showered and dressed, not really caring how she looked. Only a half hour gone by on a day she knew would go agonizingly slow. *How do I get through the morning, the afternoon, the night?* The task felt impossible, but she dragged herself through the day. She did not do it for herself, not even for Derek. She did it for her family. Her mother had lost her own sister to cancer just four months earlier. Valerie knew her mother was grieving over her sister's passing as well as Derek's, and she didn't want to add to her concerns.

A week later she went back to college, Massachusetts College of Art and Design ("Mass Art") in Boston. Valerie went to classes and coaxed herself to be productive. She found relief in creating sculptures. To be sure, the artwork she fashioned was dark and gloomy with no sense of whimsy. She wasn't consciously trying to construct such serious work, it just happened. And it didn't really matter. What was important was that it provided a small measure of escape, allowing time to pass.

And so a pattern took hold. "I would get up in the morning, go through the routines of the day—dressing, eating, attending classes—and then in the remaining free time I'd head straight to the studio. I was well aware of my hermit behavior. And I realized I barely talked to the other students, but what was there to talk about?"

She did not regret her decision to alter her college plans a year earlier and attend Mass Art instead of Syracuse University. It had given her more time with Derek, and now the art studio was providing a tenuous lifeline.

A couple of people prodded her to "move on" with her life. Valerie felt they had no idea what they were talking about, and certainly had never been through anything similar. She wouldn't move on because she couldn't, nor did she really want to.

Somehow Valerie made it through the long winter months.

She and Alex saw each other occasionally and talked on the phone. They didn't talk long but Alex was perhaps the one person who knew almost exactly what she was going through, and she appreciated the contact. She spoke with her parents of course, and they offered love and support. And those were about the only people Valerie talked to. She had drifted away from her high school girlfriends even before Derek died, simply because she spent every free moment with him. And when a couple of friends did reach out to her she couldn't really engage them in conversation because she didn't want to be a drag on them and couldn't relate to what was happening in their lives. Besides, being a recluse and a workaholic was accomplishing what she needed: getting through the days, the weeks, the months.

That summer, however, brought a change. She went to Paris on a scholarship to continue her studies. It was a difficult thing to do at a time when she felt so fragile, so alone. The new surroundings did provide some welcome changes, if only in scenery, because she still worked around the clock. But it was hard being in a new place and not able to share the experience with Derek, her best friend. She wondered if it would always be this way, if she would always feel alone and like an outsider.

ℛ ℛ ℛ

Alex Abrams was having his ups and downs, mood swings and blue moments, but not the continual void and ache Valerie was experiencing. Like Valerie, however, he too altered his college plans out of his love for Derek. About a month before Derek died, he decided not to return to the University of Pennsylvania for the spring semester, but instead registered for two courses at Harvard

University in nearby Cambridge so that he could be closer to Derek. The two young men had spent a lot of time discussing college, going all the way back to Derek's early acceptance at Tufts University, at about the time he initially started feeling sick. Alex recalls how confusing that period was

"When Derek first felt ill he didn't want everyone to know he was sick, because even he wasn't sure what was happening. He stayed out of school quite a few days, and rumors were going around the high school, some as far-fetched as claiming he had flunked out of school. When he finally learned it was cancer, he asked me to tell the coach of the basketball team we both played for. That was difficult. But one of the lowest moments for Derek was when he later realized he would not be able to go to college the following September because of all the cancer treatments scheduled for the coming months and all the uncertainty."

At Swampscott High School the vast majority of students go on to college, and discussion of college intentions with your peers is a big part of senior year. With Derek's college plans on hold he felt cheated. He was on the cusp of having all these new experiences and adventures when the illness forced him to postpone college.

Alex knew how hard it was for Derek to watch everyone else go off to college, which is why it was a tearful goodbye when Alex left for Penn in September. "When I went to school it felt weird," says Alex, "and the challenge for me was dealing with two worlds at once, and the real dichotomy between these worlds. For example, I'd go to a fraternity party and I'd see people stressing out about which fraternity they wanted to be in or who knows who, and I'd think, 'This is a big deal to you?' These people are in drama over the most inconsequential things, and I'm thinking my friend is seriously ill with cancer at eighteen years old."

Although Alex tried not to let Derek preoccupy his thoughts, that's what was happening. And when he'd call his friend on the phone and tell him what he was doing he felt almost guilty because he knew those were the things Derek wanted.

In October when Derek took a turn for the worse, Alex was really afraid. Alex was an optimist by nature and he tended to believe that Derek would eventually beat the cancer, figuring that at most his friend would miss a year of college. But in October even the best doctors in the world weren't quite sure what was happening, and this forced Alex to confront a new scenario. For the first time he contemplated that his friend might not make it. Even Derek's phone calls to Alex took on a different tone. Throughout the illness Derek had tried to put on a positive face, attending class functions when he could, such as participating in the senior show and speaking at graduation. But now that uplifting personality was being worn down by the illness. Alex would ask Derek how he was and Derek would tell the truth. "I'm not good. I'm sick. I'm tired. I'm depressed."

Alex was devastated. He was a freshman away at college trying to make new friends, but he needed a level of support these new people just couldn't give. They had no idea what he was going through, they were just too young. Most people that age had never been this close to illness. Alex felt he was living in the college world but his mind was in Swampscott with Derek, and he just couldn't be in both worlds. He ultimately decided to take some time off and be back near Derek.

He also contemplated his own mortality. Alex had always been interested in film, and now he was thinking, *I could die at any moment, I should be following my passion and making movies right now.* He thought about dropping out of Penn, and after taking the two courses at Harvard perhaps he would enroll at Boston University, which had an excellent film program. He discussed this idea with Derek, but Derek thought he was being impulsive, and didn't want his friend to abruptly leave Penn. The last thing Derek wanted was for Alex to do what Valerie had done and give up the dream of going to college in a new area.

Later in the fall doctors informed Derek that his cancer was terminal, and he in turn told Val and then Alex. Alex's mind went into overdrive, struggling to comprehend what he'd been told. He had known older relatives who died, and even people near his own age who died suddenly. But to have his best friend tell him he was dying was almost too much to bear.

Derek died on the day Alex began his classes at Harvard. He was walking home from the train he had taken into Cambridge and when he reached his house his mother was waiting on the front steps where she broke the sad news. Alex thought of how profound it was that Derek had passed away on the first day he started at Harvard. It was as if Derek was saying, *See, I really didn't want you to change your college plans for me. Live YOUR life.*

Alex's decision, however, proved to be a blessing. Living quietly at home and commuting to Harvard was what he needed to decompress from the ordeal. Had he returned to Penn he wouldn't have been able to handle the typical crazy scene at a dorm or a fraternity. Instead his days were relatively uneventful, using the time on the train to listen to music, relax, and try to make sense of the last twelve months. Of course there was no sense in what happened, and each night he would dream about Derek.

But during those train rides he found a bit of peace. One day while on the train he smiled to himself with the revelation that his big decision to leave Penn with the idea of helping Derek ended up helping himself. *Maybe*, he wondered, *Derek had something to do with that.*

ℛ ℛ ℛ

Peter and Sandy had been divorced for ten years when Derek first became ill and they faced this difficult situation. The challenge, however, was not entirely new because their oldest son Bryan had been diagnosed with severe depression, and the two parents were doing their best to get him the proper treatment. In fact, during Derek's illness Bryan was living at a residential treatment center in Vermont, and the Sheckmans were juggling care for both their sons.

Bryan was seven years older than Derek. Perhaps because of the age difference Bryan was very protective of his younger brother, and the two boys had a close relationship, with their parents' divorce making it even closer. The brothers would put on intricate performances for family and friends where Bryan was usually the "DJ and Lighting Manager," and Derek the performer, usually doing dance numbers to songs by Michael Jackson. They also played sports together with Bryan teaching Derek the ropes. They especially loved basketball. "When Derek played against bigger kids," recalls Bryan, "he had no fear. He really was an amazing athlete. It was actually kind of funny looking back on it, because in his early years I'd grudgingly allow him to play basketball with me and my friends, but then there came a point where he was better than me! That's when our games became competitive."

Sandy recalls how Bryan would go out of his way to teach Derek new things, such as playing the guitar. "Derek really looked up to Bryan, and Bryan was just delighted to have a younger brother. Before Derek was born Bryan used to ask us on a weekly basis when he was going to get a brother. So when it happened he made the most of it."

The respect and admiration between the brothers was mutual. "It wasn't just Derek looking up to me," says Bryan, "I looked up to him as well. He could do some things I couldn't. He also had a way of attracting friends that most people could only wish for. I think people sensed his giving nature and wanted to be around him. They would gladly let him lead because he was fair and so open."

When Bryan went off to college it not only separated the two boys physically but it was also the beginning of a much larger divide. This was the time when Bryan first showed signs of depression and began to withdraw. Shortly after Bryan's graduation from college the illness became more serious, and he was diagnosed with major depression, and he also suffered some psychotic episodes. Although he was not schizophrenic, he also sometimes suffered from paranoia. This is when Peter and Sandy realized he needed around-the-clock care, and Bryan was admitted to the treatment center in Vermont. Just a few months later Derek was diagnosed with cancer.

Hearing about Derek's tumor was yet another blow for Bryan. "It was so hard to deal with. I wasn't able to communicate like I wanted to. I was so out of it I wasn't fully aware of what Derek was going through. And then he was gone. My poor parents had two major burdens to deal with." Bryan wished it could all be different, but in many respects his illness was as debilitating as Derek's, as it robbed him of his ability to function like he wanted to.

Both Sandy and Peter were grief-stricken when Derek died, but their remaining son needed them and they simply could not allow themselves to shut down. They did not withdraw, but they did allow themselves to grieve. Peter, a doctor with a specialty in infectious disease, has a unique view of grief: "I think of the brain as a physical organ damaged by grief as if struck by a baseball bat. Healing of such an injury is painful and slow. The pain is present upon awakening in the morning and worsens as the day goes on, as contacts and reality frame the loss." Healing, Peter thinks, can only come with time, the same way that a broken leg heals, only longer.

Friends and family members are what got Peter and Sandy through the darkest months when they were mourning for Derek and were anxious for Bryan. "My friends simply refused to leave me alone," says Sandy. "And equally important, I allowed them to help." Sandy continued her work as the assistant director at the local Jewish Community Center, and that helped get her out of bed in the morning. But some challenges seemed too much to handle. For months she had been planning to lead an interfaith trip to Israel, but now, just two months after Derek died, she decided not to go. Again her friends stepped in and encouraged her to make the trip, knowing the combination of activity and being around other people was what she needed. Sandy hesitated, but finally let herself be talked into making the excursion. "That trip was such a good thing," she recalls, "especially because I was with caring people. Part of the reason I went is because Derek taught me to be open and let it happen."

Close friends, family members, and concerned people were also the reason Peter went back to work at the hospital just two weeks after Derek's death. "I was lucky I had a lot of people around me—hundreds of patients knew of Derek. I welcomed their kind words. Colleagues were wonderful as well. They covered for me when Derek was ill whenever I took time to be with him, and now they rallied around me." Peter also forced himself to stay physically active and found solace in his orchestra group from which he had been absent during Derek's illness. Like Derek, he found comfort listening to and playing music.

Nothing in life is more difficult than being a parent and watching your child slowly succumb to an illness you are powerless to stop. Peter and Sandy had days so dark they are beyond words, but the two refused to fall completely apart. They could not retreat from Bryan, so they made frequent trips to Vermont to be with him. Nor could they forget the way Derek fought on, and they would do the same.

Chapter 3

Discovering the Journal and the Beauty of a Video

ALTHOUGH DEREK WAS GONE HE LEFT BEHIND SOMETHING THAT THE special people in his life cherished and celebrated. The journal. Each person's reaction to it was a bit different, and its later impact also depended on the individual.

No one had seen a single line from the journal, but those close to Derek would often see him typing on a laptop. Sometimes he would be propped up in bed, using what strength he had, pondering the right words to peck on the keyboard. So much had been taken away from him, but the journal was something all his own, still in his control.

Derek didn't talk about what he was writing, and no one knew if the journal was five or fifty pages long. His loved ones only knew the journal was extremely important to Derek and that it was his outlet, especially since the illness forced him to spend so many hours alone, cut off from most of his peers.

When Derek died his mother Sandy hesitated before printing the journal. "I was worried I would hit one wrong key and it would be erased. So I called my friend Anne, who was more computer literate than I, and together we printed it. I started reading the pages as they spit out of the printer, absolutely amazed at how long and detailed it was." She had the feeling that at first her son was writing just for himself, but later as he became more ill it seemed he saw the potential of the journal to have a bigger impact.

As Sandy read the later pages she realized Derek was becoming more like a teacher, wanting to share what he was learning from experience. *He wasn't going to go out quietly*, she thought. It wasn't until she got to the end that she realized the journal spanned exactly one year, and could only wonder about the significance of that.

Derek's father, Peter, was the next person to read the journal. He was a little taken aback that he didn't know his son had devoted so much time and energy to the journal. He was especially proud that Derek, at just 17 years of age, had the foresight to document what was happening to him. "I also didn't know Derek could write like that," recalls Peter. "The journal has real depth, and as it goes on it becomes more philosophical." During those first few months after Derek was gone Peter found it comforting to take the journal to Derek's gravesite and read it there. It was a peaceful spot, and Peter felt close to his son.

Derek's parents shared the journal with Alex and Valerie a few days after they first read it. Alex read it in one sitting. It was as if Derek were still speaking to him, reminding him of what was important. Alex was not surprised by its content. He had seen Derek evolve from a boy to a wise individual, as if he were someone much, much older. Physically, Alex saw the same thing as well: his friend's strong athletic body morphed into that of a very old man.

Alex thought, *This is pretty amazing, there is absolutely no BS in this journal. He only talks about things that matter, and he focuses on how you treat one another.*

To this day Alex still rereads the journal, asking himself how the words, the messages, the advice, relate to his life right now. The journal prods him to give serious thought to his current situation and reflect on whether or not he is living up to his potential, and whether he is treating others in the very best manner possible.

Valerie, like Alex, had wondered what Derek was writing in the journal. When she was handed a printed copy she was nervous with anticipation: here was a way for her to reconnect with Derek, here was a tangible piece of him to hold onto. She raced through it, looking for her name, hoping to feel something directly from Derek himself. "I was a teenager and self-involved," Valerie recalls, "and of course I wanted to see what he said about us. It was gratifying to see how he felt about our relationship but also some disappointment because there was so much more he wasn't able to write about."

Valerie got in the habit of reading the journal entry that was written on the same day of the same month one year earlier. She was curious where they were and what they were doing one year ago to the day: maybe even relive a little of the moment. She carried this ritual on for a second year as well. "There was a contemplative quality from reading of the things we did, and what Derek was thinking at the time," she muses. "But finally after two years I just had to put it away. Everywhere I looked there were reminders of Derek, and I realized that reading his words every day was not helping me heal."

Bryan read the journal about six months after Derek died, and he was particularly moved by the amount of positive entries in it despite the battle his brother was facing. "I would read it from time to time to feel closer to him," says Bryan. "Reading about all the things he wanted to do in his future that he knew would never happen hit me especially hard. He had so much he wanted to accomplish and so much to give."

ʀ ʀ ʀ

Peter and Sandy Sheckman honored Derek's wishes that the journal be made available to anyone who was interested. Within a couple weeks of his death they had hundreds of bound copies printed and made available. The reactions from readers was overwhelming. Some people called them up in tears, saying how powerful and moving it was. Several friends and colleagues who read the journal said they also had their children read it, explaining that the journal put things in perspective and opened a dialogue between parent and child.

Peter later read from the journal at some of his talks at the hospital to make the staff aware of and more sensitive to patients' experiences.

The journal, while intended to educate the rest of us and share some insights, was a way for Derek to let off steam, describe his innermost feelings that he couldn't articulate verbally, as well as a means of leaving something of himself behind. During Derek's ordeal his options kept shrinking, but the journal was his one bit of control. Something he, and only he, controlled. Derek always wanted to be an architect and he was a creative person, and these daily writings were just what he needed. In the following years, the journal proved to be a gift to a great many people, a reminder of what is important; a beacon showing the way to a more satisfying life.

ʀ ʀ ʀ

Alex embarked on an ambitious project to both fulfill his passion for making movies and to leave something lasting about his friend. He made a video about Derek. "I was thinking about the video even while Derek was alive. It was cathartic to start collecting images of when he was healthy as a way to get away from the cancer." When Derek died, however, the project not only took on a sense of urgency but also extracted an emotional toll. Each time Alex found a new video clip of his friend he would break down and cry. But he never considered abandoning the project because he knew the video was a means to celebrate his friend when he was strong and happy. His mission was to make sure the cancer did not define what Derek was all about, and through the video he wanted to make Derek accessible.

"He's not really a jock, not a nerd, not the class valedictorian, but a kid other students can relate to," says Alex. "Derek was one of those guys that could fit into any group. He didn't have the easiest life even before the cancer. His parents got divorced, his brother was ill. He had the problems all of us have. So I wanted to show him as a regular guy and help connect him to the people interested in his story."

About four months after Alex began the project he showed the finished video, first to Peter and Sandy, then to his own family as well as Val. A week or two later it aired on the local cable station so that all those who knew Derek could watch.

The video is simple and beautiful. Its magic is due in part to Alex's care and skill crafting it, and in part because Derek's kind and gentle spirit shines through. And for those who knew of Derek's ordeal it was a wonderful thing to see him having fun.

Alex's tribute doesn't hide the cancer, but it doesn't dwell on it either. Instead Derek is shown during mostly happy times, followed by a few courageous moments as he rises above the cancer and is involved with his senior year activities. The viewer doesn't see the trials Derek went through chronicled in his journal, but instead meets Derek the athlete, the leader, even the comedian. An eighteen-year-old who is comfortable in his own skin.

The video starts with a song from the Beatles titled "In My Life," with the poignant line, "In my life, I love you more." Still shots of Derek, from a little boy through high school, roll across the screen. The words "To My Best Friend" appear on the screen. The photographs give way to video of Derek giving a youth leadership presentation, then playing guitar at a high school talent show as he sings another song by the Beatles, "You've Got to Hide Your Love Away." Between lyrics Derek flashes a quick smile, clearly relishing his brief time on stage.

Next is his trip to Israel, where Derek is outdoors rappelling, riding a camel, swimming, mountain climbing, and more. The Cranberries' song "Dreams" plays with its lyrics, "Oh my life is changing every day, in every possible way," and the film progresses to a clip of Derek really enjoying himself as a coach of a girls' flag football team.

Perhaps the segment that says the most about Derek is when he is playing in a varsity basketball game. He gets fouled and goes to the free throw line. His first shot clangs off the rim. He takes his time and carefully shoots his second attempt and misses that too. An opposing player grabs the rebound, looks down court for an open man and makes his pass. From beyond the picture frame Derek streaks back into view and somehow steals the pass, and, as he's falling out of bounds, makes a behind-the-back pass to a teammate who immediately passes to an open man, who swishes the shot. It's classic Derek, not giving up. He makes something positive happen from his missed free throws.

Next is a school skit where Derek and friends are dressed up as the Spice Girls, dancing on stage as the audience cheers. This is followed by Derek playing the guitar with a large group of fellow students on stage all singing "Stand By Me." Valerie is by his side.

Near the end of the video Derek is at the podium for graduation ceremonies. He has lost all his hair, but he is upbeat as he sends his fellow students off into the world, saying, "We get ready to go on to the next step of our lives."

Then the film transitions to a photograph of Derek in the newspaper. It was the picture with his obituary. We know he is gone. A song from the musical *Rent*, "Seasons of Love," begins to play, with the lyrics, "How do you measure a year in the life?" Alex doesn't end the film here, but instead scrolls back through brief clips of Derek smiling, singing, living life to its fullest before the screen fades and the film ends.

Chapter 4

The Next Few Years

ALEX DID RETURN TO THE UNIVERSITY OF PENNSYLVANIA IN THE FALL AFTER Derek's death. He was trying to incorporate the things he had learned and experienced over the last eighteen months into his current situation at school. *Should I just have fun? Should I work as hard as I can?* He had learned how tenuous life can be and he eventually arrived at the conclusion that he should simply take advantage of each day. And so he incorporated both fun and hard work into each week at school. Knowing that life can be short, he made a list of things that he wanted to accomplish and even laminated it so that he would look at it every day to see how he was progressing. He felt fortunate that Derek and his journal helped him put together a value system at such a young age. "I thought," recalls Alex, "I've got this new wisdom, now don't go mess it up."

He made new friends, but his best friend Derek was always in his consciousness, and he found himself wanting to talk about his experience with Derek. "Friends would be talking about the usual things, pleasantries really, and I'd find myself saying, 'Let me tell you about my friend Derek.' I wanted to share what I'd been through and what I learned, but I was afraid of overwhelming them." He would observe fellow students and adults alike making big deals out of the trivial, and decided at that young age not to waste a moment on insignificant things. When unimportant things reared up to distract him, he simply ignored them and moved on to what was important.

In a sense, Alex was adjusting to his new reality. He had just gotten a crash course in wisdom and life at a young age, but knew that his peers had not. And so, like Valerie, he always felt a bit different than the other students. He found himself wanting to educate his new friends on some of his insights, but not alienate anyone by getting too serious. But overall, his college experience was a good one. Although he took some film courses at Penn he felt his strengths were more analytical than creative, and upon graduation he enrolled in law school, later becoming a lawyer and a banker. He also married and is the father of two children.

"Today I've incorporated everything I learned about my experience with Derek into my life. My values, my parenting, and how I care for the people around me. I decided I wasn't going to take one thing for granted, not one little thing. I use what I learned when I need to make a difficult decision."

When Derek died the Sheckmans gave Alex their son's ID bracelet. Alex still wears it today.

ɣ ɣ ɣ

The large house in which Derek and Bryan had grown up was much too big for just one person. It was now the autumn after Derek's death and Sandy knew she should sell the home, but the thought of moving was too overwhelming. Acquaintances who had children going off to college talked about being empty nesters and how their homes seemed to echo, but Sandy thought to herself, *Off to college? What about off to death? My son is not coming back.*

Despite such private reactions, Sandy asked friends to treat her the same as before Derek's death, not wanting them to be afraid to tell her news about their own children. Of course she knew she wasn't the same, knew she was vulnerable, but she didn't want anyone's awkward feelings to limit their conversation or drive them away.

While she grieved for the loss of Derek, she worried about losing Bryan too. Sandy visited Bryan often in Vermont, and did her best to manage her anxiety by immersing herself in her work as assistant director at the local Jewish Community Center. Her friend Anne was one constant companion who helped her during this difficult time. The two women had both enjoyed running together for years, and even when Derek was ill they ran every morning that Sandy wasn't with Derek at doctor's appointments or with him in the hospital. After Derek died—with Anne's gentle prodding—they continued their morning runs, talking as they ran through the streets of Swampscott. The physical repetition of taking step after step was soothing for Sandy, as was the daily routine of knowing that rain or shine, Anne would be ready to run with her. It was important to have a good chunk of each day planned in meaningful activity.

As Thanksgiving approached, Sandy steeled herself for the pain she knew would come during the holidays, followed by the anniversary of Derek's death in January. However it was the unexpected reminders of Derek that hit her hardest, such as a wedding of a friend's son. At the wedding reception when the mother and son danced together it was too hard for Sandy, and she had to quickly leave the celebration. She wondered if she'd ever be able to attend another wedding.

During the next year Sandy was promoted to executive director of the Jewish Community Center. The job challenged her in a positive way, but like Valerie, she realized that she was working incredibly long hours to run away from the feeling of loss. This kind of running, so different than the physical running she did with her friend Anne, was exhausting yet Sandy instinctively knew it was beneficial in that it allowed time to pass more quickly.

Regaining her life was a slow and painful process for Sandy. She continued her visits with Bryan, stayed close to her best friends and parents, and with other volunteers coordinated the Derek Sheckman Teen Leadership Award, given annually by the Jewish Federation. In 2003 Sandy mustered the courage and energy to sell her house. She battled the inertia that keeps so many of us from making changes, and looked for a new place to live, finally selecting a small condo on the ocean.

The move wasn't easy. After working all day she would come home to packing and sorting. *What to keep? What to give or throw away?* There were so many physical reminders of Derek, and she was reluctant to let any of them go. Night after night she would tackle the project, promising herself she would never accumulate anything again. The difficult job paid off, and looking back Sandy now says, "It was probably one of the best things I could have done for myself. If surroundings can be helpful to one's soul, that move was perfect."

Shortly after the move, other events helped her outlook, most notably Bryan's gradual improvement, meeting new friends, and travel. In 2006 she thought she could manage slowing down the pace and she left her "overtime position" at the JCC. Yet she was petrified of what would happen. Would those free hours allow new emotions of loss and grief to emerge? Somehow, she had begun to understand change was a part of life, and there were other ways to help others. And so she left her director's position and used some of her newfound time to work at a part-time position while also volunteering in the community. To her surprise, she felt relieved once the change was made and found that she no longer needed to run so fast.

Around this time Alex invited her to his wedding. She thought about the event with a hint of trepidation, remembering a previous wedding where her emotions got the best of her. But now she was used to stepping out of her comfort zone, and she attended the wedding, feeling genuinely happy for her son's best friend. And she smiled when she read the printed wedding program. Along with the bride and groom's deceased grandparents, Derek's name was next to theirs to be remembered on such as a special day. The gesture was a healing one; she knew Derek was not forgotten.

Time has allowed Sandy to absorb the painful ordeal of losing Derek and reflect on what she learned from it. "I look at life differently now," she says. "I have grown from thinking that I would never be bothered by the insignificant, to realizing that life has important insignificant moments... a kind of healing in its own way. I'm also a much more tolerant person."

Sandy recalls a saying her father used to help her through her loss. "My Dad told me, 'It's not what we get, it's how we deal with what we get.' And I've tried so hard to grow from the experience. I now know to leave nothing unsaid. Don't wait. Tell the people around you how you feel."

҂ ҂ ҂

Peter was living with his girlfriend Linda in a three-story condominium in Marblehead when Linda was diagnosed with ovarian cancer. *Not again*, Peter thought. He had lost Derek, was dealing with Bryan's mental illness, and now he was back to the heartbreaking tribulation of watching Linda slowly lose her battle to cancer. There were the frequent trips to Massachusetts General Hospital, the side effects of chemotherapy, and the horrors of watching a loved one battle with pain. All brought back memories of Derek's struggle. Added to his worries, Bryan was now living in the basement apartment of the condo, still trying to find a solution to his depression and still trying to find his place in the world.

For some, these challenges—coming on the heels of losing a child—might have been too much for one person to bear. But Peter never cracked, and instead endured. He kept a full schedule as a doctor, knowing that helping others was his salvation. His experience with Derek and Linda, he felt, made him a better doctor, giving him a greater sensitivity and depth for what seriously ill patients go through. Peter often found comfort in Derek's journal, reading a few pages from time to time to stay close to his son.

For three years Peter cared for Linda, but the cancer progressed and eventually took her life. Peter's one solace was that she was able to remain at their home through her illness. She passed away peacefully with loved ones around her.

Once again Peter's friends stepped up, refusing to let him withdraw. They made sure he knew that he was not alone and invited him to their homes and activities. His involvement with music and the Boston Philharmonic Orchestra with many close friends there provided great emotional support as well. One of his friends was a nurse named Maryanne. They had known each other for many years, going back to their work at his HIV clinic, where they always gave each other great support. Later their paths crossed again when Maryanne was Derek's hospice nurse. Maryanne's husband then became ill with terminal bladder cancer and Peter was his doctor.

Now Maryanne and Peter, who had both lost loved ones, renewed their friendship, each with a clear understanding of what the other had gone through. In time, the friendship turned to something deeper, and in 2005 the couple married. After six years of sadness there was joy in Peter's life again.

It would be easy to say Peter is a stronger person because of the issues he faced, but that would not be quite right. He was a strong person before the deaths of Derek and Linda. Those experiences, however, did have a subtle change on Peter's perspective on life, love and friendship.

When he now hears people complaining about the trivial he tries to point out all the good things they have in their lives. Many of his patients already practice this philosophy of "proper perspective." Knowing about Derek or Linda they catch themselves when they complain and say, "I can't believe I'm complaining knowing what you've been through." Peter often responds by reminding them that their concerns, worries or health issues are important and are not diminished by another's experience.

Friendships, Peter knows, are the key to surviving difficult times. Whenever he felt like withdrawing, friends were always there to keep him active and engaged. "I knew my friends were important to my healing, because I witnessed the way Valerie and Alex stayed close to Derek," says Peter. "They were extraordinary. We adults could learn a lot by emulating the true friendship that Valerie and Alex showed."

Peter has used Derek's journal in teaching his staff about the personal patient experience, and is considering using the journal in his teaching of hospital residents and new physicians in the community. "We teach medical science and diagnosis and so on, but we don't teach or share what we have learned about death and dying. We need to be able to talk about these difficult issues."

ℜ ℜ ℜ

About six months after Derek's death Bryan was able to move out of the residential treatment center. Doctors had finally found a mix of medications that partially stabilized him. Sandy and Peter helped their son get a small apartment in Montpelier, Vermont, where he received out-treatment therapy. In a few months he found work at a radio station in Burlington, and relocated to an apartment there, where he lived with two understanding roommates. Soon he was working at two radio stations owned by the same company, where he thrived, and the success helped rebuild his confidence.

His recovery however was not without setbacks. Bryan worked for over two years at the radio stations but was let go when his ratings started to slip. Luckily, he soon found work mixing audio and performing other production tasks for live television newscasts. But a year later the stress of the job caused some of the old paranoia to return. He left the TV station and moved back to Swampscott where he lived with his father while continuing to work with doctors on finding the right medications to combat his illness. "My progress was two steps forward one step back," recalls Bryan. "It was not a smooth recovery or a straight path to getting better. I was lucky my parents stood by me and that I found the right therapist."

When he was feeling better he enrolled in graduate school at American University to study international relations. But again a bout of depression threw him off track and forced him to leave school and move back with his father.

Just when it appeared the pattern of improvement followed by setback would be a permanent one, things started to fall Bryan's way. His chemical imbalance was effectively treated with medication, and equally important he found a part time job as a substitute teacher. For years friends and family had commented that Bryan would make a great teacher based on the way he nurtured and shared his knowledge with Derek years earlier and the way he interacted with younger people in general. He never took the advice to heart, but now he would find out if that was true.

Over the next several months he substituted where ever there was a need. One of the administrators at a middle school he was teaching at suggested he investigate an opening for a permanent substitute. This time he acted upon the advice and secured the position, thinking that this would help him decide if teaching was truly the right fit. It was. He enjoyed the work, and especially liked teaching social studies, and after a year he found a full time job as a high school history teacher. A year later he settled into the job he has now, teaching middle school geography.

His life got even better in 2006 when he met Mandy. "Even though I was still living with my father, she saw something in me. On our first date I picked her up in my mother's car!" As the couple got closer, Bryan began to tell Mandy about his brother, eventually sharing the journal with her and visiting Derek's gravesite. And a year later when they got married, the couple asked Peter and Sandy to read some of the journal at their wedding ceremony.

Bryan now realizes that part of his illness was thinking the bad times would never go away. Even though people told him things would get better he didn't believe them because he couldn't remember how he felt before the depression. But he learned that positive affirmations really did help him, and that the more he told himself he could do a certain thing, the more he felt he really could. And so he pushed on.

"It was a jagged path to where I am now. Everyone has to find their best path, and you just have to hang in there until you do. This sounds like a cliché, but I learned time is a healer. Sometimes you have to wait it out. Fake it until you make it. It's ok to pretend." He also realizes he had an opportunity that Derek did not. "I realized I was alive and that I had a chance for some good things where my brother did not. We all have this amazing freedom. We don't know what's going to happen or who we are going to meet, but because we are still here we have the chance for great things. I'm so happy I chose teaching. I feel I can make a difference, even if it's just one student. And now I feel real empathy for students who are going through troubled times, and I try to help, try to draw them out. That's a result of both Derek's and my experience with illness."

In 2008 Bryan and his wife became the proud parents of a baby boy. They named him Derek. "I can't wait," says Bryan, "to tell my son about my brother."

※ ※ ※

Valerie was back at Massachusetts College of Art for the fall semester and continued her pattern of working long hours in the studio. She did, however, start riding her bike on a regular basis and felt that continued exercise was essential to keeping her spirits up while forcing her to get out of the house. Soon she started jogging as well. She also visited Alex at Penn, but without Derek's presence the dynamics of the friendship had changed and she felt she was just slowing down Alex's healing.

It wasn't until her junior and senior years that she started socializing a little more. While working at a part-time bakery job she got to know one of the customers and they began dating. It was the first person she dated since Derek's death and it was a big step in emerging from her solitary routines. The bakery position also opened up another door to Valerie, introducing her to the art of making pastries.

Upon graduating things were looking up for Valerie. There still wasn't a day that went by when she didn't think of Derek, but time had lessened the initial pain. She cobbled together several part time jobs including teaching art in an after-school program for the Boston Public Schools, working at the deCordova Museum, and as a waitress. She soon found a job at a bronze foundry, making commercial rubber molds of original pieces of art. One project that especially excited her was working on a monument to the 2004 Olympics in Greece.

In 2002 Valerie decided to move to New Orleans with a man she was dating. The move offered a chance to reinvent herself where nobody knew her history. Although the relationship with the new boyfriend didn't last, Valerie loved New Orleans and her work as an assistant to a talented bakery chef. For the first time since Derek's death, she felt free, felt brave, and even somewhat invincible. She was becoming her own person again—learning new things in the culinary field, meeting new people and exposing herself to a life so different than the one she knew.

Although she still thought of Derek every day, her contemplations were different now. There was no desperation. Instead of dwelling on missing him, she thought more and more of the good times they had shared and the love they had. She began to appreciate the last months she had with him. It occurred to her that so many people lose loved ones suddenly and never have a chance to say how they truly feel, never have a chance to ask the most intimate questions. With Derek, Valerie had ample time to talk and share innermost thoughts. They discussed difficult topics such as how life for Valerie might be after Derek was gone. She now felt thankful that she and Derek had left nothing unsaid, and told each other how much they loved each other over and over again.

Valerie was also grateful for her new found sense of confidence in New Orleans. She had her own apartment, new friends, and work she loved. She was thriving and on her own, figuring things out in her own way. New Orleans was beginning to feel like home.

Then Hurricane Katrina took aim at her city. Valerie heeded the warnings of officials and those of her parents and left the area days in advance of the storm, heading back to Massachusetts to visit her family for what she thought would be a week's stay. But while driving her truck north, sleeping in rest areas to save time, she listened on the radio to reports of what Katrina was preparing to do to New Orleans. Once in Massachusetts she watched television and could not believe the scenes of devastation the hurricane had caused. Whole sections of the city were under water or swept away, and with great sadness she knew her job and the new life she created were gone. It was another tough blow; just when her life was looking up and contentment seemed within reach, it was all snatched away. She felt adrift: her friends in New Orleans were scattered and she had lost touch with her friends in Massachusetts. She didn't even contact Alex or the Sheckmans while in Massachusetts, thinking that if she were to continue to heal she needed a break from her past.

A month after Katrina ruined the city, Valerie drove back and saw the damage first hand, fighting back tears as she collected her few possessions. There was no work in New Orleans, and at the urging of a friend she visited Aspen, Colorado. There she landed a job at the Little Nell Hotel. She enjoyed the work, but found the atmosphere of the resort community quite different than her beloved New Orleans. Gone was the laid-back lifestyle, replaced by long seven-day work weeks in the glitzy resort community. She felt tired almost all the time, and attributed it to both the effects of the high altitude and the grueling restaurant schedule.

Valerie met a guy in Aspen who was also a seasonal worker on the mountain, and they were soon a couple. She had finally shed the habit of comparing every man to Derek. She knew it was unfair for any boyfriend and unfair to herself because it would keep her trapped in the past. It didn't mean that Derek had left her thoughts, but she was able to compartmentalize her feelings for him and not let them dominate. Yet she still couldn't fully open up with someone new, and felt she would never find the best friend she had in Derek.

Her new boyfriend was originally from St. Paul, Minnesota, and when the winter ski season was over he asked her to return with him to his hometown and look for work there. In Minneapolis they decided to buy his deceased grandmother's fixer-upper that they thought they could restore, live in, and possibly sell for a profit. Soon Valerie was back to working seven days a week, splitting her labor between the house restoration and a position with a catering company. She was happy with her boyfriend, and although rehabilitating the house together was a big step, Valerie felt something was missing. But she was simply trying to live in the moment and find her place in the world.

The exhaustion she had felt in Aspen, which had abated a bit, returned, only this time it was even more pronounced and she noticed her skin was easily bruising. Rather than see a doctor she ignored the signs of trouble and continued to push herself, grinding through each day of work. But one day excess bleeding from her menstrual cycle was too much to ignore and she had her boyfriend take her to the local hospital's emergency room. Doctor's were concerned enough to keep her in the hospital.

Just hours later, Valerie received the life changing news that "something was wrong with her blood." One week later she was diagnosed with Myelodysplastic Syndrome (MDS), formerly known as "preleukemia." This blood disorder manifests itself in the stem cells of the bone marrow and can be fatal.

Suddenly Valerie's world was turned upside down yet again. She was told that in order to have any chance at survival she would need a bone marrow transplant, and it would have to be done immediately. Valerie thought of Derek, and his unsuccessful surgery to remove the tumor, and knew that even with the transplant there were no guarantees. It was the cruelest turn of events: that Valerie was now ill and would be undergoing her own grueling regiment of treatment.

The transplant was performed at the Fairview Medical Center at the University of Minnesota in Minneapolis. She was too ill to be flown back to Boston, but luckily the Fairview Medical Center was one of the very best hospitals for a transplant. For two months Valerie was kept in isolation, with her only visitors being her immediate family, a family friend and her boyfriend.

Valerie's mother, who flew out from Boston and rented an apartment across the street from the hospital, was her primary source of strength and encouragement, staying with her daughter every day. Her sister also moved to Minneapolis to care for Valerie and help her mom, and her father flew back and forth as often as possible. Her brother, who was her bone marrow donor, left his wife and newborn son to spend time in Minnesota to make the transplant possible. The entire family rallied around her. And every bit of their love and support was needed as Valerie was given massive amounts of drugs to keep her alive, and she had to fight through several life-threatening complications.

Time seemed to crawl at the hospital, and Valerie spent much of it thinking. She reviewed the last couple years of her life, and she didn't like who she had become. There was too much anger, too much detachment. Day after day she thought about her personality, her actions, and the way she dealt with people. She knew that she had shut out many people from her life and had not let anyone new fully enter it. She thought those decisions were because she had not let Derek fully go. *If I ever get out of here I'm going to do this life better. I'm going to do whatever it takes to heal physically and emotionally. I've got to let my best friend Derek go and let new people into my life. No one will ever take his place, but I need to value others in an entirely different way.*

Her boyfriend's visits became less and less frequent, and each time he came he was more distant, the conversation more forced. The illness frightened him and Valerie sensed that he simply did not have the inner resources to be helpful. In fact, his presence made an incredibly difficult situation even harder. Valerie was in survival mode. She needed support, and her boyfriend simply couldn't give it. She decided to give him a way out of the relationship. "I knew that I was going to be sick for a long time, and I wanted him to go live his life. He was not a bad person, but he just couldn't deal with the situation. It was too much."

At the end of two months Valerie had improved enough that she was released from being an inpatient at the hospital. Still, for the next month she was required to return for transfusions and monitoring every day. At the end of this period, she was flown to Boston where her monitoring would require a once-weekly session at a local hospital.

Moving back was difficult. Valerie had grown used to the safety of hospital life and familiar doctors, nurses and other patients. In Boston she would have to start all over again. She didn't know anyone anymore. She had no friends. Her hair had fallen out from the effects of her treatment, her weight had increased by 45 pounds from the steroids used to fight the rejection from the transplant. Whenever she went out in public she wore rubber gloves on her hands and a mask over her nose and mouth to guard against germs while her immune system rebuilt.

Valerie also worried about how her return home impacted her family because she was still very ill, some days feeling so weak she could only stand up for a few minutes at a time. She often needed help with some of the simplest tasks. Gone was the total independence she had enjoyed in New Orleans and Aspen, replaced by a dependence on others. Yet in a surprising way this new dynamic offered her a different kind of freedom. She was no longer detached, no longer as guarded, and more open to sharing feelings with others. In a cancer support group she learned that all her experiences from the days of Derek's battle with cancer to the present, allowed her to assist others in coping with their illness and the limitations it placed on them. By helping others she was helping herself, and she was following through on her promise to "do this life better."

Valerie released her residual anger from losing Derek, as well as anger over her own condition. It had been suggested to her that her illness might have been triggered by exposure to chemicals in the workplace during her time at the foundry. Although she talked to lawyers, they said it might be difficult to prove a connection based on the short amount of time she worked with the chemicals. The old Valerie might have pushed the fight, but now she realized the important thing to do was to focus her energies on living rather than battling insurance companies. She wanted to move ahead, not backwards.

During the next year Valerie regained some of her strength. Yoga sessions were a big part of her recovery, helping her feel a sense of empowerment. She developed an attitude of "tomorrow I will be able to do more than I can today," and that forward type of thinking gave her a quiet confidence. She used Facebook to reconnect with old friends. "I went from no communication with people," recalls Valerie, "to using this amazing new resource to share and celebrate the good news of my recovery with a whole group of friends. I would post entries like, 'Today I was given a three month reprieve from the Dana Farber Cancer Institute!' I wanted to scream it out, and Facebook let me do that." She also used Facebook to watch some of her friends' children grow up, because she couldn't see them in person due to her compromised immune system.

After a year and a half, Valerie felt well enough to look for a part-time job. She longed to be a productive member of society. "I didn't know if I could ever work again, and I was scared, but I had to try." She interviewed at a high-end bakery business and during her discussion with the owner Valerie told him about her illness. Rather than be wary, the owner of the business was understanding and warm; he looked beyond her limitations, recognizing her determination. Valerie was hired as a part-time pastry decorator and she gave the job everything she had. Sometimes after working a five-hour shift she would return home and sleep for almost two straight days. But that was a small price to pay for the satisfaction that came from being productive.

Over the next two years Valerie slowly regained her independence, increasing her hours and responsibilities in her job while moving to her own apartment. Joy and happiness had returned to her life.

Derek is still a part of Valerie, still residing in her heart and mind. His memory no longer holds her back, but instead makes her happy. And sometimes his spirit seems incredibly close. "I get a lot of beautiful signs from Derek, things that seem to be beyond coincidence. I don't fight it anymore or try to read too much into it, but just enjoy. I used to hold onto these as the most important things in the world but now I just think they are gifts. I think this is the way the universe works and I'm going to go along with it."

Chapter 5

Full Circle: Buck Harris and the Journal

FOUR YEARS AFTER DEREK'S PASSING, BUCK HARRIS, A HEALTH TEACHER AT Swampscott High School, was cleaning off a shelf in his classroom when he noticed a copy of Derek's journal. A memory came back of a tall, thoughtful student, who had become ill during his senior year. Buck had Derek in one of his classes that year, and he wished he had gotten to know the young man better. But that was the first year Buck taught health at Swampscott, and his teaching style at the time was quite traditional, which allowed for limited genuine connections with students.

Buck wiped the dust from the journal and carried it back to his desk, intending to read a few pages. An hour later he finished the entire journal and stayed seated, looking out over his empty classroom, deeply moved. *Can I possibly use Derek's journal in class?* he wondered.

Buck had read the journal before, when the Sheckmans first gave the school a copy. That reading had been painful, coming too close on the heels of Derek's death. This time, however, Buck saw the journal in a new light. Here was a document filled with wisdom and lessons learned, and best of all it was told by someone who was the same age as the students Buck taught each year.

Buck contemplated how he might use the journal in the classroom. He had evolved as a teacher during the last four years; his classes were more informal with an emphasis on discussion and reflective writing. No longer afraid to take chances, Buck realized the journal offered a unique opportunity, and he tried an experiment in the classroom the next week. He had the students arrange their chairs in a circle with lights lowered, and then take turns reading the journal aloud with periodic breaks for discussion. "Never had I received such significant and thoughtful responses," recalls Buck, "as I did from using the journal. It moved and inspired students to carefully examine their own lives."

Buck later asked the students to write about how the journal impacted them, and most students said the journal caused them to make a change in their own lives, particularly in how they interacted with others. Here is an example from that first class:

Last year was the first time that I heard of Derek Sheckman. All I knew was that he was some kid who went to our high school and died of cancer. I did not know that he could ever have any real effect on my thinking or my life. I was wrong. When Mr. Harris said that we were going to read his journal I was really excited. I thought it was just a documentary that Derek kept about his struggle with cancer. It was that, but also so much more.

One paragraph really stuck out to me. He said that we should never hold back our feelings, and not be afraid what we want to say to others. We should do this because who knows when you will ever get the chance to say it again. I never thought of this before I read Derek's journal. I know I have held things back because I was afraid to say them. I never want to regret not saying something to someone. I never want to look back on my life and regret anything. I want to know that I did everything I could. We only get one chance to be here.

Derek's Gift

I do not want to dwell on things that happened in the past, but instead start living in the present. We need to appreciate the time we have, and how we are now because things change. We cannot wait until later to start living. I really want to thank Derek Sheckman for opening my eyes.

Buck was especially surprised by this essay because the person who wrote it was shy and hardly said a word in class, yet her reflection on Derek's message showed insight and thoughtfulness that had not been expressed before. On the basis of essays like this one, and the intense classroom discussion, Buck considered his teaching experiment a success. The journal was going to be a permanent part of his teaching. Yet, there would be risks.

Buck began to see that the journal served as a conduit for some students to open up about their personal problems, some serious. Sometimes a student's reaction would be to say, "I'm not doing so well." The student might have problems at home, problems at school, or depression. Some teachers advised Buck not open a can of worms, others said students shouldn't have to deal with death at so young an age, and one college professor even told him that by teaching Derek's journal he was stealing the innocence from students.

Buck consulted with a friend and colleague named Lori Hodin, a psychology teacher. Lori, like Buck, was one of Derek's teachers, but she knew Derek far better than Buck (she wrote Derek's college recommendation.) She remembered Derek as someone who took his school work seriously, but also as a young man who was easy-going around fellow students, with a mature and innate kindness. During his illness, Lori had a session in class where students presented a "show and tell" about childhood.

Each class member brought in an item, such as a Teddy bear, to talk about what it had meant to them. Derek, who was undergoing chemotherapy treatment at the time, brought in a corner of his old blanket. He explained how his "blanky" helped him as a kid, and was now helping him again as a teenager enduring chemo. "He was open about his illness," recalls Lori, "sharing what he was going through, sharing what he was learning."

After Derek died, Lori read the journal, and wasn't surprised that it was full of life lessons. She thought Buck's health class was the perfect place to bring it to life and unleash its power. She recognized that Buck wanted to inspire students about the importance of building relationships and thought he should go ahead and stick his neck out, and use the journal as a teaching tool. After all, Derek wanted the journal to have the widest audience possible, although he probably never dreamed it would become part of his high school's curriculum.

And so over the years Buck continued to use the journal as a way to prompt students to think about relationships. He expanded the discussions to explore resiliency and mindsets for overcoming challenges, while also encouraging students to consider the "what ifs" in their own lives. Lori and Buck would brainstorm about the teaching application of the journal, and Buck would tweak his techniques, but he kept the essentials of reading the journal out loud, having the students discuss it, and then later put their thoughts on paper. "Buck really appreciates teenagers," says Lori, "both their hearts and minds. He provides a safe space in the classroom where students can reveal and disclose who they are: the good, the bad, and the ugly."

When students voiced serious problems, Buck became adept at helping them find the right resources and professional help to guide them through their personal storm. This was essential because the journal, as well as other lessons, opened up dialogue in the classroom about serious issues. Besides the talk of peer pressure, depression, and drugs and alcohol use, some students talked about family matters such as their parents' divorces or a serious illness. One student talked about his father beating his mother, and another about the murder of a family member. Buck never knew what the journal might trigger, but he was aware it was the vehicle to encourage some students to think and discuss issues that are rarely talked about. And he saw students giving helpful advice to one another, something Derek would have been proud of.

"Kids today are electronically distracted," says Buck, "and they have an insatiable need for contact on a constant basis. That's why they are always texting. But the contact they are having is pretty insignificant. When I teach and use Derek's journal it gives the students an outlet to talk about some things that are bottled up inside them. That can be a first step toward healing or getting help, or maybe making a change in the way they live." Buck has read the journal probably more times than anyone, and he still picks up new insights. He never knows what to expect from each group of students; some connect with Derek and his messages far more than others, but every student has been moved by the journal and its power for introspection. As a health teacher, Buck considers it a success whenever a student examines the way they live and the decisions they make.

ℛ ℛ ℛ

Being a high school teacher is not for the faint of heart. During

Buck's first year of teaching he quickly realized that students often arrive to class moody, distracted, or withdrawn. Many view the teacher as an interruption in their social life. A teacher, Buck learned, wore a variety of hats, far beyond instructor and motivator. Author Frank McCourt wrote that in the high school classroom "you are a drill sergeant, a rabbi, a shoulder to cry on, a disciplinarian, a singer, a low-level scholar, a clerk, a referee, a clown, a counselor, a dress-code enforcer, a conductor, an apologist, a philosopher, a collaborator, a tap dancer, a politician, a therapist, a fool, a traffic cop, a priest, a mother-father-brother-sister-uncle-aunt, a bookkeeper, a critic, a psychologist, the last straw."

That first year Buck recognized that getting and keeping a student's attention was no easy task, and he found a more informal approach to teaching kept the students engaged longer. Then when he started using Derek's journal he felt his teaching entered a whole new level. He could see how students fell out of their roles and began an unfiltered, even vulnerable dialogue. Although it was the journal that got the students to open up, Buck's facilitation of the discussion created the atmosphere where students felt free to discuss the most gut-wrenching topics. He would set the tone by listening, asking questions that were insightful but not prying, and establish norms of non-judgmental response so students who did talk freely would not be ridiculed or laughed at. And he asked that what the students say be kept private within the confines of the classroom. He was amazed how students honored these ground rules, and how even the class clown, loudmouth, or domineering personality would be humbled by the journal and show a sensitive side.

Students were breaking away not only from their roles, but

from their comfort zones. And although difficult for some, all remarked how the class sessions revolving around the journal were unlike any other high school experience. Even the students who could not find the words to express their feelings verbally poured out their emotions in the reflective writing exercises. Buck knew that the introspection he was seeing was because Derek's journal set the bar high; it provided a powerful example of teenage reflection that motivated the students to thoroughly examine their own lives.

Buck decided to write to Peter and Sandy Sheckman and share what he was witnessing. He closed his letter by writing, "I only wish I had started using Derek's journal in class years ago." Peter Sheckman wrote back to Buck. "I have often wondered whether anyone other than family and a few friends would ever read Derek's journal again. I am so pleased that your students found value in it.... Continue to use the journal for your classes... it makes me feel good to know that his life has continued meaning."

Buck later met with Derek's brother Bryan, who was substitute teaching in Marblehead, a town that borders Swampscott. Bryan gave Buck a more complete picture of Derek's personality than the journal provided. The two teachers discussed not only Derek and his relationship with Bryan, but also Bryan's recovery from mental illness and his new teaching career.

Buck wondered how he could incorporate the more complete picture of Derek that Bryan had painted. He felt that was the one thing missing in his teaching of the journal. He needed the students to see that Derek was a lot like themselves, and not a stranger reaching out from the past. He wanted the students to really feel Derek's spirit and visualize what he was writing about. The answer came in a surprising way when fellow teacher Tom

Derek's Gift

Reid mentioned to Buck that Derek's best friend Alex Abrams had made a video about Derek shortly after he died. Buck's eyes widened: a video would be far better than anything Buck could have added about Derek's personality. He watched the video that day and knew he had found the perfect complement to the journal.

Buck considered opening his teaching session on Derek with the video, but ultimately decided to show it right after the students finished reading the journal out loud, and before any discussion started. The student response was profound. "Most often," says Buck, "the video leaves my students speechless. The film never shows Derek after his facial surgery, but instead shows him dancing, singing, playing the guitar, traveling with classmates to Israel, playing basketball, and more. For my students this makes Derek more 'real.'"

One student's essay is typical of how the film affects the class:

> *I am a visual person. I need to see and experience things to understand them. As we read Derek's journal I comprehended it, and was moved by it, but it wasn't until watching the video that I fully grasped the whole story. It is not until I saw Derek dancing on stage with his friends, coaching the Powder-puff game, and walking the halls of Swampscott High that I believed it. And it was not until I saw the pictures of Derek's best friends with him that I cried. It is all too similar to my life right now. When I saw the video I felt like Derek was my friend that I had just lost. I could feel the same love that his friends felt for him because I felt like I knew him.*

Buck felt like he finally had the complete teaching lesson he had been crafting. But in 2007 he got a phone call from Valerie Rosenberg. Buck had sent a letter to her years earlier explaining what he was doing with the journal, but he had not heard back from her until the surprise phone call.

Valerie explained why it took her so long to respond, saying that she had recently visited Peter Sheckman who asked if she had seen the booklet Buck had assembled of student essays about the journal. "Well," said Valerie, "Buck did contact me a few years ago when I was in New Orleans, but I didn't think it was a good idea to re-immerse myself in Derek's journal."

Peter answered, "You should look at these student responses. There are even letters to you from students."

Valerie started reading the essays and letters right there at Peter's house and felt a sense of wonder. *Wow, this is exactly what Derek wanted.* She read one particular letter directed to her that made her pause and think that maybe she was ready to get involved. She felt connected to the process and knew that whatever teaching methods Buck was employing, they were the perfect match for the journal to elicit such powerful responses from his students.

Valerie called Buck and suggested they meet. The two had a remarkable conversation about her relationship with Derek, the experience of his illness and death, as well as her years after high school and her current illness and slow recovery. At the end of the meeting Valerie surprised Buck by expressing an interest in sitting in on one of his classes involving the journal. "I'd like to be an observer, at least on this initial visit," said Valerie. Buck said no problem, but he was concerned that if the students knew that Valerie was in the room that their attention would be on her and not on themselves. To avoid compromising the lesson, they decided that the students would be told that Valerie was a publisher interested in hearing the students read and discuss the journal for possible publication.

On the day of Valerie's visit to the classroom she thought she would be even-keeled because nobody knew who she was. Instead, as she listened to the voices reading Derek's words, she felt strong emotions, but managed to keep them hidden. Viewing the video, however, was a different story. She thought she would start crying when Derek came to life. She hadn't watched the video in eight years.

The whole experience was strangely both draining and energizing, but Valerie saw how valuable the process was for the students. After all, she was just a few years older than them. "I saw that the session gave the students space to share," said Valerie. "It allowed them to talk about such questions like, What does it mean to mourn? What does it mean to be afraid? And when kids are afraid how do they bring it up to friends and parents?"

When Valerie was in high school there was no outlet, no one for her to talk to. In fact, one teacher who noticed her acting a bit withdrawn while Derek was sick said, "Stop being depressed, he's going to be fine, it's not so bad." She knew that would never happen in Buck's class, and thought that his new way of teaching just might ease the heartache some students might be experiencing. At least, she thought, they would have a safe place to express themselves either verbally or in essay form. She decided that during the next session she would talk to the students and do her best to tell her story, her journey, in the hopes that it might help others. Buck suggested they videotape the session so that future classes could have the same benefit, and Valerie agreed.

Before Valerie's next visit Buck explained to the class that she would be coming to speak and answer questions. The students were blown away—it was like a character was going to step out of a book. They had just finished reading the journal and wondered what she would look like? Would she be angry, happy, or still grieving? Would she answer every question or would some be off limits? Buck suggested the students use discretion, but that he thought Valerie would be open and forthcoming, and if there was something she didn't want to talk about she would say so.

Valerie surprised herself by not only staying composed but enjoying the process, interjecting humor where she could and encouraging any and all questions. She opened the discussion by explaining that the cancer diagnosis for Derek changed her whole life. She never expected Derek to die, mentioning her sense of hope after Derek had the surgery on his jaw even though it deformed his face. Later in her opening remarks she reviewed the years after high school and explained that now she was in recovery from a leukemia-like illness and how the bone marrow transplant was grueling but successful. She confided that when she was at her lowest she thought, *How could Derek let this happen to me?* "I had looked to Derek to protect me. It took me awhile to realize he had nothing to do with it. I had to let him go. Getting sick was a turning point: I realized I had let ten years of my life go by thinking he was right there for me. So now I can speak about him without getting totally emotional. I still think about him all the time but its different now."

Valerie didn't discuss the journal per se, but instead focused on why Derek wrote it. "I think he was compelled to write because he had such creative energy. Even when the tumors were spreading and he needed morphine he still made the effort to write in the journal."

By the time the question period started, the students knew Valerie was approachable, and they didn't hold back. One young man pointed out that in the beginning of the journal Derek mentioned he and Valerie had been fighting, and he asked Valerie to comment on it. She pointed out how young they were and commitment was a new thing. "It's hard to remember that we ever fought," said Valerie, "because that was eliminated the instant Derek got sick."

Another question: "Did you and Derek have a pact to continue to communicate in the afterlife?" Valerie paused and answered that they didn't really talk about the afterlife because they were like most teenagers, focused on the present. "But Derek would have wanted me to go on and have my own life."

Buck followed this up with a question of his own, "So there was no arrangement that you two would try to connect after he was gone?"

Valerie broke into a big smile, "No, but I wish we did. What a good idea. Shoot! I totally wish we had discussed it." Then she paused and added, "But we never missed out on the opportunity to say I love you. And getting engaged was a way to show the world how much we loved each other."

Another student posed the question of why keep fighting on, after Derek's death and now Valerie's illness. Valerie responded that sometimes she asks herself the same thing. "If you ever wonder why you should stick around in this world, try to think of just one reason, or just one person to be here for."

Toward the end of Valerie's visit the group discussed the ways the journal prompted them to make changes in their lives or what part of the experience really hit home. One girl said, "I learned the value of life—how what happened to Derek could happen to any of us. We saw him on the video dancing to the Spice Girls at the Senior Skit—well, we did the same thing to a more recent song."

Valerie closed her session by saying, "Why not just tell people you love them and care about them. And then show it and do it."

After the class was over one student approached Valerie and said, "I'm so glad you are doing this. My dad had cancer and now my mom has a brain tumor. No one here talks about these things. I've had this idea for a cancer support group, but I'm not sure how to go about getting it started."

Valerie looked at the young woman and nodded. "Great idea," she said. "I'll help, let's do it." The two women got the group started within a couple weeks, and both saw how the shared experience of having loved ones with cancer or having cancer yourself, brought various people together, creating new bonds of strength. Valerie later commented, "I'm not a counselor, but I've been through enough to know you need the support of others. Helping this girl get the group started was something I felt I was meant to do."

To learn more about Buck's teaching visit: www.NortiaPress.com

Chapter 6

Derek's Key Insights

DEREK HAD MORE THROWN AT HIM IN HIS TWELVE MONTHS OF ILLNESS THAN most of the rest of us experience in a lifetime, yet he still managed to make entries in his journal. So much of his former self was stolen away by the cancer: his athleticism, his good looks, and most of his social life. He had no say over what his illness did to him physically or the limits it placed on him, and over time his sphere of control shrank and his options dwindled. But he did have command over one very important aspect of his life: his reaction to what happening. And that reaction included asserting himself through his journal. In the beginning the journal was much like a diary, chronicling what was happening to him and explaining his feelings. But over time—probably because he knew he may not beat the cancer—the journal morphed into something larger than himself. How remarkable, given his weakened state, that Derek turned the focus of his entries toward helping others lead happier, more satisfying lives.

Derek knew he would not be able to benefit from the insights he was discovering, but decided they would not go to waste. He fought through his fatigue and took the time to write what he was learning so the rest of us could gain from it. He wanted us to make changes in our lives now, rather than when we are jolted by serious illness or a catastrophic event.

Derek was not going to go out of this world quietly. He needed to leave a record of what *he was*. He wanted us to know that he was much more than his illness. And finally, he was compelled to share. Cancer might take his life, but not before his determination to contribute to the world. He had something to say, and nothing was going to stop him.

In some entries Derek implores us with a real sense of urgency to reassess our lives. *Don't wait*, his words seem to shout, start making the changes this very minute. See if you can.

It's What You Have

We tend to dwell on what's missing from our lives and overlook what we have. Derek turns this tendency on its head, and starts with the basics: it's a gift to be healthy, it's a joy to experience friendship, and it's even a treat to be able to smile. If you have one of these things you are lucky, if you have all three you are truly fortunate. He knows that taking things for granted is human nature. Before his illness he assumed he would have good health, but his experience made him want to shake this attitude right out of the rest of us, and instead replace it with gratitude. *"Appreciate what you have and understand how easily these things can be taken away."* Money had no real meaning for Derek and success was a hollow word.

We all have things missing in our lives, things we are striving for, a station in life which we think will make us complete. Some of us think that compared to others we have many gaping holes in our accomplishments, and that may be true. But the inverse is also true. Each of us has simple things that others do not, and we need to recognize those, and enjoy them. Do you feel well when you wake up? Are you able to eat your favorite food? Can you take a walk? These are just some of the things Derek reminds us are not just everyday occurrences, but gifts, blessings, and should be enjoyed and cherished. Gratitude should be part of everyday life.

Despite Derek's hardships he felt fortunate in many ways: he had a true partner in Valerie, a steadfast friend in Alex, and a family that surrounded him with love. *"My family and friends are so amazing. I am so lucky to have their constant support."*

Next time you find yourself complaining or feeling that nothing goes the way you want it, turn your attention to the things you do have. Think of Derek's message of appreciation, and how much he missed some aspects of daily life that were taken from him. *"My advice is to take advantage of the simple things."*

Give Yourself Some Credit!

We are too hard on ourselves. And when we have achievements, we seldom acknowledge them, but instead plow ahead, thinking of what's next. Some of us are hoping others may give us a pat on the back: maybe your spouse, maybe your boss, maybe your close friend. Derek didn't wait for others to acknowledge his little triumphs, he did it himself. When he finished six weeks of radiation in March, he wrote *"I am finished, and damn proud of myself."*

After Derek gave his graduation speech he acknowledged both the difficulty and achievement of standing on the stage despite being sick: *"I was able to get through what I needed to accomplish—a great feat."* And later, in October, when the disease forced radical facial surgery and a ten-day stay in the hospital, Derek found humor in the simple act of enduring. *"I believe what*

*doesn't kill you makes you stronger. If that's true, I am really,
really strong."*

𐆛 𐆛 𐆛

Self-compassion helped Derek keep sane through an incredibly
difficult time. His ability to cope was assisted by his knack for
being his own best friend. He rarely berated himself, blamed
himself, or dwelled on shortcomings, but rather recognized all his
efforts. And if he had a bad day, he showed resilience by bouncing
back the next, by showing kindness to himself the way he would
to others. He used his journal not only for sharing advice, but
as a way of talking to himself, offering positive feedback on his
triumphs, no matter how small.

Next time you achieve something important, or even just see
an obligation through to its conclusion, acknowledge what you
did. Don't worry if no one else notices; the best praise is from
your toughest critic, yourself. Anytime you can say, "I've done
my best," know that success or failure measured by others pales
in comparison to your own knowledge that you *tried*. Too many
people don't even attempt something difficult because they are
afraid of failure or concerned of what others might think. To those
people, Derek would probably shout, "Go for it! Don't ever hold
back!"

Say Something!

We all wonder what to say when someone has a serious illness
or is brokenhearted. And that awkwardness causes some people
to avoid the sick or the grieving. We worry we will say the
wrong thing. To combat this inclination, remember that there

is something far worse than saying the wrong thing, and that is saying nothing.

When Derek was first diagnosed with cancer and word spread through the school, he wrote that students didn't know what to say or how to act. Some tried to treat him *"normally, while others tended to shy away."* Derek understood that people didn't know how to act around him because it was a new situation and it was *"foreign"* to them. He related a story of a childhood friend who had cancer in elementary school, and how friends pulled away from the sick child. Derek worried that now he was in the same boat and people *"would look the other way."* That was the last thing he wanted. *"I hope my friends will stay my friends."*

The awkwardness of not knowing what to say is no excuse for ignoring the person or pretending everything is normal. Speak from the heart. If you see an acquaintance fighting a disease try saying, "I heard about your illness and I just wanted you to know I'm pulling for you." Or "praying for you," or "thinking of you"— the point is it doesn't really matter how the words come out; the person will know you care. Silence is complicity; silence empowers the illness and not the person. Silence can be interpreted to mean you don't care or you are too busy to take the time to let the person know your concern. Acknowledge reality.

If you are prepared to do more than letting the person know they are in your thoughts, say so. You might say, "If there is anything I can do, just let me know." It's natural to think there's nothing you can offer when someone is fighting cancer or serious illness, but let the friend be the one to make that decision. They might just surprise you by saying, "you're one of the few who has asked," or "Thank you, yes, I could use a ride to my next doctor's appointment."

In several different journal entries Derek makes a point of explaining just how important people's gestures of caring or the giving of one's time can be: *"They are calling. They are writing. They are cooking. I love them for it. That is the truth."*

ϟ ϟ ϟ

Derek got a cold lesson about looking "different" or having a deformity. When he first lost his hair and eyebrows from the chemotherapy he wrote that he felt like he was branded with a sign that said, *"He's sick, so stay away."* That was the last thing he wanted. Friends could have said, "How are you feeling?" If the sick person wants to talk about it in detail they will. If they don't, they won't. But it's important that you asked, because that is what the ill person will remember. You don't need to bring up the person's illness every time you see them. Once you have broken the ice and expressed your concern, friendship and perhaps the gift of your time, is what matters. Inclusion—rather than moving away out of awkwardness—is the way to go. Derek was included in the senior events, such as graduation ceremonies, the prom, the senior skit, and those were some of the happiest days in the last year of his life.

The same theory holds for how we treat people who are grieving. Derek's mother Sandy recalled how after Derek's death a female acquaintance in the grocery store saw her and scurried away. The woman probably didn't mean to be rude, but rather she didn't know what to say and panicked, taking flight into the next aisle. All she needed to do was approach Sandy and quietly whisper her condolences. Then she could have waited for Sandy's response. If Sandy merely nodded, the woman could have ended the conversation by saying, "If you need anyone to talk to, please call." Or if Sandy struck up a conversation about how difficult her days were, the woman could have offered to meet for coffee, take a walk together, or any number of ideas that would show she cared enough to give of her time and include Sandy in it.

Ducking into the next aisle is unacceptable. It just makes the grief stricken person feel even more alone.

The "say something" approach can be expanded to everyday life, and everyone you meet—a new student, a clerk at the convenience store, or a secretary on the phone. Go beyond just saying hello and ask a question. Next time you're at a restaurant ask the waitress what dish she likes, or ask if she likes working weekends or weekdays better. People appreciate a little attention. Who knows, your comment, your interest, might just make the person's day, help them relax, smile or change a bad mood into a good one. Say something.

Tell Them How You Feel

After Derek was told in December that his cancer was terminal one of the recurring themes in his journal was his advice to tell special people in our lives how strongly we feel about them. *"Do not wait to tell someone how you feel about them. Do not wait for the right moment."* He is all too aware that if you don't verbalize your feelings the person may never really know how much you admired them, loved them, or the effect they had on you. He goes on to prod us to be specific with our feelings for others. *"Tell someone in your life that you appreciate them—give them a compliment—it will go a long way."*

Although Derek suffered considerable pain and discomfort because he did not die quickly, there was one silver lining: he had the opportunity to let his loved ones know they meant the world to him. They would never have to wonder if they had done all they could for Derek, he told them they did.

To underscore those feelings that he verbalized, he also expanded upon them in the journal. He knew that after he was gone everyone would read the journal and they would be reminded once again of their impact in his life. For example, Alex and Valerie would never have to second-guess themselves on whether they had done enough for Derek. He makes it clear that both were helping in ways that brought him to tears. He even wrote that they were doing too much, that they should focus more on their own lives. Derek wanted his friends to move on after his death, to have no regrets about their commitment, and no doubt about just what they meant to him. With Valerie, Derek backed up his words of love with the engagement, while Alex would always know Derek loved him like a brother.

Imagine for a moment that right at this instant you drop dead. How many important thoughts about others would go unsaid and would go to the grave with you? It would be awful if people close to you never knew the impact they had on you, never knew the depth of your love. Even beyond your inner circle of friends and family, there are likely other people who are clueless of their importance in your life. It might be a teacher, a teammate, a mentor, a neighbor. You don't have to get all emotional or sappy, a simple acknowledgement will do: "My life is so much better because of you"; "You have been the best neighbor a person could ask for"; "You have no idea how much your advice helped me."

Don't assume people know how you feel. Tell them.

It's Ok to Be Angry

When something really bad happens, it's ok to be angry. You can't put a positive spin on things that truly hurt. Derek had his moments of anger, such as his entry just six weeks before his death, *"I am filled with so many emotions. I am filled with rage and anger –why me? What did I do to deserve this?"* Of course he did nothing to bring on his suffering, and who wouldn't be angry at being dealt such a hand? Derek's anger was his will to live. It didn't mean he was in denial, but on the contrary he knew the reality of his situation, and his anger was his assertion that he got a raw deal. As much as possible he tried to stay positive, but Derek was honest enough to acknowledge he was afraid, confused, and frustrated. He didn't add to his burden by thinking he was a weak person because of these feelings.

His frustration needed a voice, and by writing it down and also expressing those feelings to Val, Alex, and his parents, Derek found a way to vent. Venting means to release, and Derek seemed to intuitively know that if he didn't articulate his resentment over the injustice that had befallen him it would become toxic and consume him.

Anger is cited as stage two of the five stages of grief outlined in Elisabeth Kübler-Ross's book *On Death and Dying*. She points out that anger is a necessary step in the healing process, yet our society puts a premium on suppressing anger. Derek seems to have found a way to balance this strong emotion by expressing it in his journal. The simple act of acknowledging his anger through the written word was a way to let steam off in a measured way rather than having it explode. (Interestingly, Derek does not fit neatly into the chronological stages explored by Ross: Denial, Anger, Bargaining, Depression, and Acceptance. Derek encountered some of these in a different order, and Derek largely ignores the bargaining stage, where people say things like, "I'll do anything for a few more years." Instead, he showed strong coping skills, which are outlined in the next insight.)

Derek searched for meaning in his adversity. Often he couldn't find it, and this kept the anger simmering. Later in his ordeal, however, he started to craft his own meaning and response to his situation. He might not have been able to control the cancer but he could help others by sharing what he was learning in hopes that all those who read the journal might benefit in some way. He channeled his anger and frustration into the energy required to clearly and eloquently write his opinions and counsel. He was angry and productive.

Throughout the ups and downs of Derek's illness he knew he was doing his best, and he never felt guilty over his days of anger. If you do your best you will never have regrets. Some days Derek's best was simply getting through the day, hour by hour, not wanting to talk to anyone. Other days he'd show his fighting spirit. Without the anger Derek may not have ever written his journal.

ᛉ ᛉ ᛉ

Positive thoughts can do wonders, but Derek is a great example that even a naturally upbeat person can't overcome the resentment that comes from random accidents, illness, or just plain bad breaks. When something terrible happens through no fault of your own it's logical to be angry. Derek showed us that when anger rears its ugly head, acknowledge it, and let it pass through, and do your best.

When anger persists, or depression takes over your every

waking hour, reach out to counselors, spiritual advisors, or friends. Derek opted for the latter, and Val and Alex understood—after all, they were angry too! They were losing their best friend.

Focus on Others and the Power of Purpose

In several sections of the journal Derek's concern is not for himself but for others. It would be understandable if this eighteen-year-old was completely self-absorbed, but throughout his ordeal he is aware of other people's lives. If he is worried about a friend or family member he either tries to help or expresses his concern. Examples include his father's break-up from his live-in girlfriend, his brother's illness, Valerie switching the college she was going to attend, and Alex wanting to transfer from University of Pennsylvania to Boston University to be closer to Derek in his final days. (Derek makes a keen observation about Alex: *"He is mixing up his devotion to me with what he wants in his life. I think it would be best for him to return to U Penn."*)

Derek's concerns were always out of love, but focusing on others helped divert his attention from his own bleak future. When you are busy helping others you forget your worries. And in times of depression, illness, grief and other difficult periods any relief is welcome, even if just for short periods of time.

It's easy to obsess about your own troubles, but take time each day to think of the challenges other people face, and see what you can do to help. Derek made this part of his daily life, and on occasion, even used it as motivation to keep doing his best, to fight on. For example, in regard to his brother Bryan's depression, Derek looked forward to the day when the two of them felt better and could just sit and talk. He couldn't help his brother while he was battling cancer, but down the road there might be opportunities. In May Derek wrote, *"He [Bryan] is one of my driving forces for getting better. He needs me just as much as I need him."*

Of course Derek's desire to help others extended to people he didn't even know. His journal entries advanced from diary-like recordings of events and feelings, to passing along insights gained so others could take full advantage of their lives. He was basically saying, *I may have had to suffer to gain these nuggets of wisdom, but I want others to benefit while still in good health.*

Long before the phrase "bucket list" became popular, Derek had his list, but with a twist. In his final months he knew he would die soon, so he hoped that friends or family would be able to do a few of things on his list. He wanted them to either think big (*"write a classic novel"*) have fun (*"jump out of an airplane"*) or make a lasting impact on someone else's life (*"get one person to quit smoking"*). Derek's bucket list was clearly written to get every reader of his journal to take time out from their day-to-day life and do a few things out of character. He implores us to take action that will cause us to feel accomplishment, joy, or just to laugh about.

ℛ ℛ ℛ

Derek couldn't go off to college or start an occupation, so he created his own career: keeper of the journal. It kept him productive, and gave him a sense of purpose. He obviously felt that if his journal helped just one person, all the effort he put into his writing would have been worth it. It's a great lesson for the rest of us: staying busy, having a sense of purpose, and focusing on others can help us get through our own difficult times.

Derek instinctively knew that if your time is empty your mind will fill the vacuum with self-worry. But by writing, Derek showed his resolve to be constructive while at the same time offering the rest of us a path for better living. You too can fill a void through writing, cooking, working at an animal shelter, exercising, volunteering at a hospital, tutoring, or any endeavor that provides diversion. And the best activities are those that not only entertain you but also help others, even if indirectly.

So forget yourself for a few moments by remembering others.

Live in the Moment and Prioritize

Of all Derek's messages this is the one that is the easiest to grasp and the hardest to follow. We often live in the future. When we do that we are giving up the sure thing (today) for the unknown (tomorrow). Some of us even live in the past, replaying old wounds, failures, and "what ifs." By doing so we miss opportunities in the here and now.

Over and over Derek reminds us to enjoy the journey, enjoy the good things and people in your life. It's great to have goals—Derek certainly did—but he learned that waiting for some distant pay-off over the horizon is ludicrous if you are not enjoying the path taking you there. You may not make it to your ultimate destination, so feel gratitude for the here and now, and have a sense of satisfaction for the steps you are taking to reach your objective. Happiness, Derek realized, should not be dependent on an outcome, but instead be an ongoing state of mind tied into the journey. The Roman poet Horace expressed Derek's message this way:

Happy the man, and happy he alone,

He, who can call today his own:
He who, secure within, can say:
Tomorrow, do thy worst, for I have lived today.

Derek's transformation to live in the moment also gave him a fresh outlook on priorities. He began to understand what was truly important in his life and what was superficial and not worth his energy. As early as his second entry in the journal he is starting to put this wisdom into practice when he thinks about a couple arguments he has had with Val: *"All of a sudden, everything we have been fighting about is unimportant."*

As the cancer spread Derek narrowed his list of priorities, noting that what was really essential included love, treating others with kindness, making the most of your time, and enjoying the present. Even some of his bigger goals, like going to college, no longer held the importance they once did. Derek knew it would not be the end of his world if he missed a year of college. He had learned a truth all of us should take to heart: our worries need to be put into the context of our total life experience. When we do that we just might realize half our worries are unimportant or don't really matter.

ℛ ℛ ℛ

Steve Jobs, founder of Apple, echoed Derek's sentiments in a commencement address he gave not long before his passing. "Remembering that I'll be dead soon is the most important tool I've ever encountered to help me make the big choices." Jobs pointed out that so many things that people think are of consequence fall away in the face of death, leaving only what is truly important.

And like Derek he hammers home the message to follow your heart, and not what is expected of you.

Derek realized he had wasted some of his prior time; *"I was doing everything I was expected to be doing."* He encouraged Alex not to fall into this trap, writing, *"He should do what he wants to do and not what he is expected to do. Life is too short."* Jobs essentially said the same thing: "Your time is limited, so don't waste it living someone else's life." Both men, through confronting death, realized how to prioritize, how to focus on the essential things, and how to block out the inclination to follow the herd. If you are busy doing what you think is expected of you, you are squandering your time, postponing what is important, and giving up today.

As time was running out for Derek and he sensed death was near, he reiterated the importance of carpe diem—seize the day—by reminding us to *"live life to the fullest, now."* It's a message we have all heard repeatedly, but how many of us actually make the conscious effort to practice it on a daily basis?

Questions for Discussion

1. In Part III of *Derek's Gift*, the authors discuss some of the key insights gleaned from Derek's journal and they also draw conclusions from the lessons learned. Do you disagree with any of their findings? Did they overlook a key lesson?

2. It must have taken real discipline for Derek to write in his journal when he was feeling physically and emotionally drained. What do you think were some of his motivations for putting such efforts into his writing?

3. Is there something you wish Derek wrote more about, or explained in more detail?

4. Imagine your best friend is in Derek's situation. Could you do the things Alex did, would you do anything different from Alex?

5. Imagine you were Derek's girlfriend Val. Could you have done what Val did? Would you have done anything different?

6. Val and Derek considered themselves to be soulmates. Do you believe in the concept of soulmates?

7. Imagine one of the special people in your life died suddenly, this very instant. Is there anything you would regret not having done or said?

8. Derek realized so much of our time is wasted worrying about things that are trivial or inconsequential. What did you waste time and energy on this year, this month, this week, that you now know was not worth the effort? What techniques can be used to prioritize what is truly important in your life?

9. Derek warns us all not to do what is "expected" of us, or do what we are "supposed" to do. Do you feel pressure to meet others' expectations, or are you following your own path?

10. If you could speak to Derek or Val, what would you want to say to them?

About Michael J. Tougias

Michael Tougias (pronounced Toe-Gis, hard g) is a versatile author and co-author of 21 books. Two of his previous books, *A Storm Too Soon* and *Overboard!* received critical praise because of their fast-paced style and "heart-pounding" narrative. His best-selling book *Fatal Forecast: An Incredible True Tale of Disaster and Survival At Sea* was hailed the *Los Angeles Times* as "a breathtaking book...[Tougias] spins a marvelous and terrifying yarn." An earlier book, *Ten Hours Until Dawn,* a story about a sea rescue during the Blizzard of 1978, was selected by the American Library Association as an Editor's Choice: "One of the Top Books of the Year." Tougias also co-wrote *The Finest Hours: The U.S. Coast Guard's Most Daring Sea Rescue,* which the Disney Corporation is bringing to the big screen. Henry Holt Publishers has released a young adult version of the book.

On a lighter note, Tougias's award winning humor book *There's a Porcupine in My Outhouse*: *The Vermont Misadventures of a Mountain Man Wannabe* was selected by the Independent Publishers Association as "The Best Nature Book of the Year." The author has recently teamed up with his daughter and written another humor memoir titled *The Cringe Chronicles: Mortifying Misadventures with My Dad.*

Tougias has prepared slide lectures for all his books, including *Derek's Gift*, and his lecture schedule is posted on his website at www.michaeltougias.com (Organizations can contact him at michaeltougias@yahoo.com.) The author also has stories on his blog michaeltougias.wordpress.com, and he has an author page on Facebook at "Michael J. Tougias."

Through research into dozens of survival stories, Tougias has also prepared an inspirational lecture for businesses and organizations titled *Survival Lessons: Peak Performance & Decision-Making Under Pressure.* Interested organizations can contact him at michaeltougias@yahoo.com.

About Buck Harris

Buck Harris is a veteran high school teacher who has been using Derek's journal in his classroom for the last ten years. Derek was a student in Buck's health class when Derek first learned of his tumor. It wasn't until several years after Derek's passing that Buck began teaching the journal in his contemporary adolescence classes (Buck describes Derek as the real teacher). Spending a week reading the journal aloud, discussing it and doing reflective writing has become a right-of-passage prior to graduation for students at Derek's alma mater Swampscott High School. This experience has stimulated powerful discussions and written reflection—many students describe it as the most important experience in their high school experience.

Also by Michael J. Tougias

Rescue of the Bounty: A True Story of Disaster and Survival in Superstorm Sandy (co-author Douglas Campbell)

The Cringe Chronicles: Mortifying Misadventures with My Dad (A Memoir, co-written with Kristin Tougias)

A Storm Too Soon: A True Story of Disaster, Survival and an Incredible Rescue

Overboard! A True Blue-Water Odyssey of Disaster and Survival

Fatal Forecast: An Incredible True Story of Disaster and Survival at Sea

Ten Hours Until Dawn: The True Story of Heroism and Tragedy Aboard the Can Do

The Finest Hours: The True Story of the U.S. Coast Guard's Most Daring Sea Rescue (co-author Casey Sherman)

Until I Have No Country: A Novel of King Philip's Indian War

King Philip's War: The History and Legacy of America's Forgotten Conflict (co-author Eric Schultz)

Quabbin: A History and Explorers Guide

The Blizzard of '78

River Days: Exploring the Connecticut River from Source to Sea

Exploring the Hidden Charles

There's A Porcupine In My Outhouse: The Vermont Misadventures of a Mountain Man Wannabe

AMC's Best Day Hikes Near Boston (co-author John Burk)

Also by Nortia Press

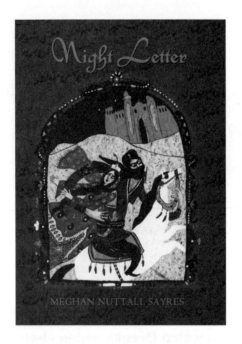

Night Letter by Meghan Nuttall Sayres

$18.99 | 312 pp. | ISBN: 978-0-9848359-0-4

Hardcover with illustrations, map and discussion guide

"Anahita's epic love story captures the mystique of long-ago Persia while providing a framework for exploring issues of social justice still relevant in our own times."
—*School Library Journal*

"The design of both books is outstanding, drawn from classic tapestries and motifs, and points to the creativity and innovative form and content that one often finds with non-corporate publishers." —*Times* Albany

"*Night Letter* is an engrossing adventure of love and danger amidst the social turmoil of early 20th-century Persia."
—Constance Vidor, Director of Library Services, Friends Seminary, New York